Temptations WOMEN FACE

F A C E

Honest talk about
....
JEALOUSY, ANGER, SEX
MONEY, FOOD, PRIDE

Mary Ellen Ashcroft

INTERVARSITY PRESS
DOWNERS GROVE, ILLINOIS 60515

InterVarsity Press is the book-publishing division of InterVarsity Christian Fellowship, a student movement active on campus at hundreds of universities, colleges and schools of nursing in the United States of America, and a member movement of the International Fellowship of Evangelical Students. For information about local and regional activities, write Public Relations Dept., InterVarsity Christian Fellowship, 6400 Schroeder Rd., P.O. Box 7895, Madison, WI 53707-7895.

Scripture quotations are from the New Revised Standard Version Bible, copyright © 1989 by the Division of Christian Education of the National Council of the Churches of Christ in the USA and used by permission.

ISBN 0-8308-1724-7

Printed in the United States of America

Library of Congress Cataloging-in-Publication Data

Ashcroft, Mary Ellen, 1952-
   Temptations women face: honest talk about jealousy, anger, sex,
money, food, pride/Mary Ellen Ashcroft.
     p.   cm.
    1. Women—Conduct of life. 2. Women—Religious life.
    3. Temptation. 4. Sins. I. Title.
    BJ1610.A76 1991
    241'.3'082—dc20   91-14233
                                  CIP

15	14	13	12	11	10	9	8	7	6	5	4	3	2	1
03	02	01	00	99	98	97	96	95	94	93	92	91		

Preface

The traditional approach to temptation has been war. Fight it; don't surrender to it; find strategies to deal with it; kill it before it kills you. What is it like when we take this approach to our temptations?

When a temptation rears its ugly head, we rush at it, blindfolded, swinging madly. We are afraid to look at it and especially afraid to ask what this temptation or sin means about who we are. Somewhere in our consciousness we hear a voice, "If you commit a sin like this—if the temptation even crosses your mind—you must be a very bad person."

We try to beat the temptation to death, but in fact we only knock it unconscious. We stuff it into a closet and pound a few nails into the door. "Well, that's dealt with," we tell ourselves. But temptation and sin monsters thrive in dark closets and will emerge larger and more threatening another time. And so we find ourselves caught in an overwhelming spiral of guilt, lack of self-knowledge, and powerlessness.

There is another way to approach temptation. We do not deny the problem but see it first as a symptom. When the temptation or sin monster crawls out of the closet, we need to stop before we bludgeon it and ask what its presence is telling us about ourselves.

Our reaction to our own temptation can be like our reaction to a child who displays some unexpected behavior, like shoplifting or smoking. Our first desire may be to shout or spank the scoundrel into submission. But that would be a shallow response to the problem. The wise parent will try to find out what this behavior indicates about the deeper needs, problems and feelings of the child.

And so with our temptations. Why do I find myself tempted by a pair of red sandals or chocolate cheesecake? Why do I find myself gossiping about a neighbor, pressuring my daughter to excel on her PSAT, or nursing a grudge toward my sister-in-law? Self-examination, understanding ourselves, is an essential step in beginning the journey toward holiness. Paul instructed the Christians at Corinth to examine themselves. When we look within, we see that often we have not examined or known ourselves or the power of our emotions.

It's little wonder that we as women don't understand ourselves. We have often believed garbled tales about ourselves. For years if we have turned to psychology or sociology for insight, we have read studies that relate more to male moral decision-making than our own. It would be remarkable if we *weren't* confused about ourselves. This confusion has made us vulnerable—and when we are out of touch with who we are and with our emotions, we are more likely to fall for temptation.

Each of us must decide how to handle temptation, and how to do it as a woman. In this book we see how the differences between men and women reveal the feminine side of the seven deadly sins. And we learn how with this knowledge we can deal firmly with sin, find true freedom, and begin to build holy and fulfilling lives.

Prologue

I met Jill shortly after she married Gavin. Jill was stunning: when she and I walked down a Seattle street, people swung round to stare at her shiny black hair, her stylishly cut clothes. I felt as if I was with a movie star. But Jill was also gentle, sensitive, and a Christian. Perhaps that was why her adultery and divorce five years later were such a shock to me and others who knew her. After the divorce became final, I talked with Jill, wondering how she understood what she had done.

Jill grew up in the South, and like most of us, learned in childhood what was significant about herself. She was a pretty child and being cute was her role. Her older brother was clever and her younger brother the baby. "When my brother was under four," Jill said, "he refused to go into the doctor's office with my mom and me. Here he was, having a tantrum, and it turned out to be because he didn't want to hear another person say how cute I was."

As Jill grew up she found her sense of identity and importance in her good looks. She became a Christian at a Baptist church, but even other youth group members appreciated her cute exterior more than her intelligence or her growing spirituality. Jill chose a Christian college to attend. There she became a cheerleader and made the honor roll; she ran around with a group of friends who went on hay rides and sledding trips together.

During her junior year of college everyone was pairing up. Jill linked up with Gavin, who was popular, good-looking, and a star student. People at the college thought they were the ideal couple. "What could be more perfect than for us to get engaged when Gavin graduated . . . so I pressured him for an engagement ring." They hardly knew one another, but she was the lovely southern belle and he was the handsome southern gentleman. They made a perfect picture, and all their friends, professors and family approved.

Jill and Gavin married and moved to Seattle. Within the first month she became depressed. She was used to having friends and family around her; now Jill began to feel lonely and trapped, with nowhere to turn for help. After a few weeks she tried to tell Gavin how she felt; he panicked. "Here we were, the darling, perfect, Christian couple from a wonderful Christian college," Jill said, "and we were scared to death."

Jill realized from Gavin's response that he couldn't understand her fear or anger or depression or longing for affection. Gavin suggested that she needed to have better quiet times. "He seemed to be saying to me that I was a bad girl, while he was the sweet, innocent man who was studying to be a wonderful Christian English professor."

Gavin refused to go with Jill to get help. Jill wondered whether she was demanding too much of Gavin. Or maybe he was just as frightened and ill-prepared for marriage as she was. Five years later they still had gotten no help.

Jill, desperate for affirmation and closeness with someone, longed for intimacy but felt rebuffed by Gavin. She had never learned to express her needs. She felt condemned at church and at home: she was bad for being materialistic, bad for not being a supportive wife, bad for wanting a career, bad for being attractive to men, bad for wanting attention from other men.

"Not that I was physically involved with anyone at that stage. But I was so desperate that I was involved in platonic relationships with . . . oh, perhaps fifty men . . . who were nice to me, attracted to me. What happened with Zavier was really just slipping further than I'd gone before in my imagination and letting it happen in reality."

Jill experienced temptation and ultimately fell into sin. Was her experience of temptation and sin different because she was a woman? Whose fault was it? The temptations which assail us and the sins we fall into are a complex mixture of what we do and what has been done to us. We can see that—in Jill's story and in our own.

PART I

WHAT'S THE PROBLEM?

1/WOMEN ARE DIFFERENT: LEGENDS & FINDINGS

My son Andrew comes to me. *"Can I go with my friends to a movie* tonight?"

My husband responds, "Have you finished your schoolwork, Andrew? You know our rule that your homework must be finished before you go out."

My response is much less clear-cut. I think about the fact that Andrew is not very sociable, that he doesn't usually ask to go places with friends. I think about friends being ultimately of more importance than a homework assignment or two. In my quandary over even a minor decision, I am displaying one way in which women are different from men.

Symptoms, Diagnoses and Prescriptions for Sin

Many psychologists and sociologists believe women are fundamentally different from men. We are different in the way we think, the way we value relationships, the way we regard ourselves. A woman who has wondered why she is more concerned with relationships than her husband and more intuitive than a male coworker may find confirmation that she is indeed different. "I felt as if I was reading something written in my native language for the first time," says Mary Stewart Van Leeuwen, a college professor, of her readings about female differences.

If we are to better understand ourselves and the temptations we face, we must pay attention to these recent findings and contrast them with the stereotypes which have been brought to us by the world. The cultural stereotypes that assail us, representing themselves as the wisdom of the world, are myths that have often burdened woman's lives.

Myth 1: Women are irrational, illogical, fickle and weak.

Common knowledge says "you can never argue with women" because they tend to be irrational and illogical. They bring their emotions into arguments and argue from human situations rather than conceptual points.

"The female sex is easily seduced, weak and without much understanding. The devil seeks to vomit this disorder through women. . . . We wish to apply masculine reasoning and destroy the folly of these women."[1] Epiphanus, who penned these helpful words, lived from A.D. 315 to 403.

Men portray women as poor decision makers, and women themselves sometimes mistakenly agree. An advertisement shows the woman who cannot decide between two cake mixes: Which one will be better for my family? This one? No, that one? Women are ambivalent, hesitating and indecisive: "It's a woman's prerogative to change her mind."

Faced with rational arguments, decisions, or traumatic situations, we simply cannot cope. For centuries we have fainted or swooned and had to be revived with smelling salts. Soap operas, cartoons and advertisements picture us as helpless, passive and unable to manage without a "superman." The weak woman myth prevails despite the fact that we are the ones who survive morning sickness, labor and childbirth and also live longer than men.

Is there any truth in this myth that women are irrational, illogical, fickle and weak? Although some women may have bought the line and acted that way, could it be that fundamental differences between men and women have led to this stereotype? Psychologist Carol Gilligan thinks so and her findings support another view of women.

Finding 1: As a woman I make decisions using different standards because different things are important to me.

Women make decisions very differently from men, according to Gilligan. In her studies of females from ten through their forties, she discovered that women, more than men, made decisions based on relationships. In similar situations men pulled out a rule book and looked for principles on which to base their decisions, while women worried more about maintaining close relationships rather than violating principles.[2]

Why would women be so different in their decision making? Psychologist Nancy Chodorow found some answers in the way children relate to their parents.[3]

Imagine the following family. John and Evelyn have twins: Robert and Lucy. When the children are small, John works long hours to provide for his family while Evelyn stays with the children most of the time. Robert and Lucy, like all little children, seek one person to depend on fully, and Evelyn becomes that person. Secure and happy, they seem to have identical upbringings.

By their second birthday, the twins discover that boys and girls are different. Daddy is different from Mommy, and it's not just that he wears his hair shorter or has a suit on. This new understanding changes how Robert views his mother. His life has revolved around her, but now she is different from him. According to Chodorow and other writers, this will confuse Robert. He knows he cannot be like his mother, his first and primary love; instead, he is meant to be like his father, a much more shadowy figure in his life. This uncertainty for Robert (and most little boys) makes his upbringing very different from Lucy's.

Robert will become less secure; he will find relationships more difficult. Throughout his life Robert will substitute other things for his lack of closeness to people—going fast on his skateboard, telling jokes with friends, playing football, excelling in school and succeeding in a profession. Robert may put women on a pedestal, but his unsureness about them may lead to a distant relationship with a future wife, or even abuse of her.

Lucy, on the other hand, has no hesitancy about her relationship with her mother. She loves her and wants to be like her. Lucy will likely be more secure and also depend more on relationships. Lucy's web of relationships will assume supreme importance in her life. When she plays with her friends, her games will be cooperative. When she goes to college, she will depend on a group of friends. Her husband and family will mean so much to her that she may endure physical abuse from her husband to keep peace.

Robert and Lucy had similar experiences, but each viewed who they were in relation to their parents quite differently.

These different values greatly affect how each makes decisions. For Lucy separation is difficult; for Robert close relationships are hard.

The different curses on fallen man and woman show this uniqueness of each sex even in the Garden of Eden.

To the woman God said: "I will greatly increase your pains in childbearing; with pain you will give birth to children. Your desire will be for your husband, and he will rule over you" (Gen 3:16). Women find it easier to rely on relationships than on themselves. Wheaton College theologian Gilbert Bilezikian sees this quality in women coming from this Genesis passage. He writes:

[The woman's] desire will be for her husband, so as to perpetuate the intimacy that had characterized their relationship in paradise lost. But her nostalgia for the relation of love and mutuality that existed between them before the fall, when they both desired each other, will not be reciprocated by her husband. Instead of meeting her desire . . . he will rule over her . . . the woman wants a mate, and she gets a master; she wants a lover and she gets a lord; she wants a husband and she gets a hierarch.[4]

Many women lose themselves wholly in the demands of others. "A result of the fall is for the male to want to exercise power over the female; the result of the fall for a woman is that she wants to sustain relationships, even if it hurts her."[5]

Myth 2: Women are frivolous, a little foolish and interested in silly things.

The idea of the foolish woman goes back thousands of years. Cyril of Alexandria, A.D. 376-444, wrote: "Somehow the woman, or rather, the female sex as a whole, is slow in comprehension."[6]

Sixteen hundred years later advertisements depict women as thrilled by their no-wax linoleum floors, ecstatic over a sparkling sink and moved by a load of bright-white laundry. Women plummet into depression because glasses have water-spots. Advertisements imply that men care about how products are made while women care about how they look. Women are vain, having time for luxurious baths while men must take no-nonsense showers.[7] Women are dizzy blondes who live to shop and are only truly happy with a new outfit and a new hairdo.

Finding 2: Women come to know things differently than men.
Is there any truth in the myth that women are frivolous and interested in silly things? Could it be that women value different things because they have come to know things differently than men?

Women may grow in their understanding of themselves and their worlds differently than men, the authors of *Women's Ways of Knowing* suggest.[8] At first they are silent, virtually unable to talk about themselves, which is a behavior sometimes seen in abused women. In the next stage women assume everyone else knows more than they and look to a higher authority for information. When women move beyond this, they may recognize for the first time that they have something important to say and refuse to listen to traditional authorities. After having their own say, they often realize they must play by certain societal rules in order to get a degree or job and so act accordingly. Finally in their journey of knowledge women arrive at a point where they are able to correlate their inner knowledge with the world outside. In moving from silence and self-consciousness to self-awareness and self-restraint, they find self-assurance.

Perhaps women who have gotten stuck at some point in their journey of knowledge have contributed to the silly woman myth. Many women have been unable to trust their own knowledge about themselves or God. They have assumed all reliable truth would come from an authority figure: the pastor, the television celebrity, a Bible teacher, or a husband. When these authority figures let women down (as anyone but God will ultimately do), women may stop listening to others.

To find health and wholeness we must listen both to others and to ourselves.

Myth 3: Women cannot reach God as men can.

Five months ago one of my writing students visited an orthodox Jewish synagogue as part of an assignment. The men around her squirmed and looked uncomfortable until the rabbi came over and whispered, "You'll need to come and sit over here." He led her to a chair that was behind a screen.

She looked at him, puzzled. "Why?" she asked.

"Because otherwise you would distract the men at worship."

Gretchen came to me upset. "They wouldn't even let me sit with them," she said. "I felt ashamed, as if I were a bad person."

"Do you know what your problem is? You are too closely related to Eve," I said. "She was a temptress, responsible for the fall of Adam as well as her own fall. You had to sit on that chair because of a long-standing fear of women within many branches of Judaism. You, like Eve, are a temptress who might lead men astray."

The Old Testament portrays two "models" of a woman: "woman as temptress" and "woman as wise and strong." Judaism and certain distortions of Christianity emphasized the "woman as the morally impure temptress." Jesus and his disciples did not ostracize women, but the church fathers forgot the example of Jesus and revived the idea that women are waiting to snare the unsuspecting man. Tertullian, who lived from A.D.

160 to 225, concluded this about women: "You are the devil's gateway; you are the unsealer of that forbidden tree: you are the first deserter of the divine law: you are she who persuaded him whom the devil was not valiant enough to attack. You destroyed so easily God's image, man."[9]

Women, shunned as temptresses, have often been told they cannot fully reach God. Origen (A.D. 185-254) wrote of women, "What is seen with the eyes of the creator is masculine, and not feminine for God does not stoop to look upon what is feminine and of the flesh."[10] Some thinkers in the sixteenth century wondered whether females possessed souls. Even today, some denominations and groups suggest that women find access to God only through their husbands or church leaders. One contemporary Christian writer asserts:

> A woman's vulnerability . . . does not stop at the physical level. It includes also vulnerability at the emotional, psychological and spiritual level. Here too, she needs a husband's authority and protection. . . . It is the husband, not the wife, who is primarily responsible for what goes on in the home, the community and the church. When he deserts this role, or when the wife usurps it, both the home and the community . . . suffer for it.[11]

Finding 3: Jesus related to women differently than others did.
Jesus did not accept Judaism's view of women as temptresses, those responsible for evil and to be avoided. First-century society kept women "strictly segregated from the social and religious life of their communities as inferior and unteachable creatures, and they were mercilessly oppressed within the seclusion of their fathers' or husbands' homes."[12]

But Jesus was a radical in his treatment of women; he invited women to follow him. He allowed them to touch him, he healed women and spoke to them. Women are part of Jesus' miracles, parables and discourses.[13] Women were the last to be with him when he died and the first to discover his resurrection. Jesus rejected the teaching of the world about women, but sometimes women have had trouble rejecting these teachings themselves.

2/TEMPTATION & SIN FROM A WOMAN'S PERSPECTIVE

Myths *about women have saturated our culture for generations.* Few people have stopped to ask how women are really different from men. Tanya, one of my students, wrote about seeing her priest concerning her marital problems. Her story is revealing.

I went to see Father Frank when I was desperate. I explained to him that my daughter was now in kindergarten and I wanted to go back to school, finish my degree and think about law school. My husband felt that my place was in the home; and to convince me he belittled me, swore at me and yelled at me. Recently he had started beating me, and I sometimes went to the grocery store trying to hide the bruises on my face or a black eye.

After I finished my story, Father Frank told me that the solution was very simple. I had taken a vow to become my husband's wife and that was all that I was meant to be. He told me that I was being disobedient to my husband by wanting to be more than a wife; my husband and daughter should give me as much feeling of wholeness as a woman needed. He said I should be thankful that I had a husband who loved me enough to want to take care of me so that I didn't have to work. Our first session was over and he told me to go home and pray.

I went home and prayed, but I kept thinking that God didn't really want me to suffer this emotional and physical abuse. I wasn't sure, but it didn't seem to me that God would want to punish me for using my gifts, yet Father Frank was telling me that this was so.

In my next (and last) session with Father Frank, I told him that I couldn't accept that I was put on this earth to deny myself totally in order to serve my husband. I also didn't feel that every time I didn't bow to my husband's smallest wishes, I should be subjected to physical beatings and sit back and take it.

Father Frank very patiently tried to explain to me that it was I who was making myself unhappy. He said that if I would get these foolish ideas out of my head and stop wishing that I was a man, then I would be happy again.

I asked him if the abuse was also my doing. He said, "Yes; you have upset your husband with your need for independence. He is trying to be a good provider and you are trying to emasculate him. This is his way of fighting back. It's only normal." He suggested that I go home and apologize to my husband, make him his favorite meal and show him what a good wife I could be.

When I told him that I wasn't sure I could do that, he told me that I was selfish; I was thinking only of myself. He told me that my main problem was ego and self-centeredness in wanting to use my gifts rather than being contented to stay in my God-given lot in life. He told me that arrogance like mine was the sin God hated most. If I wanted to stay near God and not throw away my salvation, then I would need to smash my selfishness and ego. Going home to my husband and taking whatever abuse he gave me was a good way to do that, Father Frank said. When my husband hit me, he would be beating away my selfish ego.

Why didn't Father Frank see Tanya's real need? Was he blinded by his own point of view?

Male Perspective as the Norm

For centuries both sexes have considered the male point of view to be normal in almost every area of life, from theology to art, from literature to medical science. Only within the last few years have people noticed that in an area as "objective" as medical research, males are considered to be the normal subjects. An article in *Time* magazine described two typical research projects: one analyzed heart attack prevention by using 22,071 male volunteers and another studied the effects of caffeine on 45,589 men.[1]

Some women feel that medical researchers have studied men more than women to be mean and nasty or because there's a plot to exterminate women by not finding cures for women's diseases. I don't believe this is true; male experience has simply been considered to be normal and women's experience a variation on that norm.

Just as medical research has tended to focus on men, so has

theological study. For example, male religious thinkers often describe sin through male eyes because they are falling back on their own experience. Yet a woman's encounter with temptation and sin may be radically different from a man's.

Medical researchers or theologians should not stop studying the male body or sin from the male perspective, but they should recognize the limitations of such studies. They may be doing what Paul suggested the Corinthians should not do: "But when they measure themselves by one another, and compare themselves with one another, they do not show good sense" (2 Cor 10:12). The ideal (both in medical research and in looking at temptation and sin) is a broader understanding based on the perspective and experience of the whole human race.

The Diagnosis of Man's Sin

Many male theologians write critically acclaimed books, have colleagues look up to them and students applaud them. When they write about temptation and sin, they naturally think of their swelling egos and feelings of independence from God when others praise them. They are concerned about the self that sets itself up against God and thumbs its nose at him. If this is the male theologian's diagnosis of human sin, then the prescription is simple. The self needs to be smashed. "The old, the sinful self, the self which is centered in itself, must be 'crucified.' It must be shattered and destroyed," writes theologian Reinhold Niebuhr.[2]

But what if a person's sin springs not so much from an overconfident ego as from self-loathing? How does smashing the self work in a woman's life?

Father Frank counseled Tanya by assuming that her problem was her ego. Similarly, Jill's minister couldn't see the obvious pain and disorientation that was leading to her temptation to adultery. When Jill sought help from a minister during her crisis, she told him what her husband, Gavin, had told her: "I don't love you. I don't feel a thing for you." The minister told Jill that Jesus didn't give a rip about her emotions, that she should ignore them. Jill found it impossible to ignore her pain. And she kept contrasting Gavin with Zavier who seemed to love her unconditionally. "He made me feel like a real person; he gave me the love I longed for," Jill said. "But the minister shamed me, telling me my children would be ruined, Jesus' death mocked, any future ministry of mine spoiled, my salvation put into jeopardy, the church reproached, my life ruined, my husband's heart broken . . . on and on."

This minister didn't recognize that Jill was slipping toward sin not from a defiant self-concept but from an unworthy one. Jill felt that if she listened to the minister's counseling, she would vaporize, and the little of her that was left would be gone forever.

Wrong Diagnosis, Wrong Prescription
These clergymen were assuming that male experience is normal experience, standard experience. They made a wrong diagnosis based on that assumption and then offered a faulty prescription. Many women do not suffer from too much self-confidence but from self-hatred; this fact is borne out by psychologists, sociologists and literary historians. For instance, when women write autobiographies they write them very differently from men. Women who write autobiographies have usually been highly successful in some way, but they apologize about their deficiencies and try to explain them.[3]

"To be sure, it is usually said that sin in its original form is man's wanting to be as God. But that is only the one side of sin. The other side of such pride is hopelessness, resignation, inertia and melancholy. . . . Temptation then consists not so much in the titanic desire to be as God, but in weakness, timidity, weariness, not wanting to be what God requires of us," writes Jürgen Moltmann.[4]

We can see this despair in what women write about themselves:

"It occurred to me when I started packing that it was kind of ironic. You think the important thing when you are leaving to go somewhere is that you are taking your body somewhere else and of course your belongings follow along, but it seems almost as if my belongings outweigh me because that is all there is left of me. I just feel really beaten down, lost, and I feel really tired. There seemed to be more substance to the actual material possessions that I was putting in the trunk than there was to me. I thought, 'There is more to the trash you fill your life with than there is to you.' "[5]

"There are times when I look in the mirror and want to smash it. Lots of times I feel I'm not worth walking out the door. I see myself as a really useless, small and pathetic person, basically a piece of dirt."[6]

"I don't know. . . . No one has told me yet what they thought of me."[7]

"I guess the feeling I most often have toward myself is this nagging loathing, a kind of disgust. Sometimes everything about me, especially my body, seems disgusting. Then I get even more disgusted with myself for being so filled with this self-disgust."[8]

Tempted to Fill the Gap with Other Things

If a woman feels totally unlovable, and unloved, she may fill her life with substitutes for God. To offer a woman who despairs of God's acceptance the traditional male prescription of "smashing the self" is to kill rather than cure.

When I look at my own temptations, I see that my vulnerability to them often comes out of a desperate need for approval. This need is not unusual. Perhaps it is the fact that women have been consistently devalued by the culture, or perhaps it is women's close identification with a mother who probably suffered from low self-esteem. But we see this low self-esteem on the shelves of self-help books in bookstores and libraries: *Women and Self-Esteem: Understanding and Improving the Way We Think and Feel about Ourselves, Women Who Love Too Much, Perfect Women: Hidden Fears of Inadequacy and the Drive to Perform, The Cinderella Complex: Women's Hidden Fear of Independence, Why Do I Think I Am Nothing without a Man?, Men Who Hate Women and the Women Who Love Them.* It is hard to imagine shelves of similar books for men. These books discuss various pitfalls open to women as they seek to fill the emptiness within.

Trying to Feed the Voracious Monster
The need to prove our own worth to ourselves is never satisfied. The beautiful Jill is never beautiful enough. Our inner self becomes like the mythical dragon that demands more and more maidens to fill it. We all know the feeling: "If only I could meet the right man, my life would be wonderful.". "If only he would stop drinking (or get a better job, or stop playing so much golf, or come to church), then my life would be fulfilled." "If only my daughter could get into Harvard, then I'd know that I'd been a good mother." "If only I could get the house looking like I want it to, then I'd feel great." "When I finish my degree and get the job I want, than I'll feel fulfilled." We also all know that the elation of the accomplishment lasts approximately thirty seconds and then we need more to convince us.

The monster will not be satisfied. Success may satisfy women even less than it satisfies men. Most women, when surveyed, ascribe their failures to their lack of ability and their successes to good luck.[9] (Men tend to evaluate their performance in just the opposite way.)

Women respond to self-doubt in a variety of ways. We may try to prove ourselves worthy by piling our lives fuller and fuller with things we know we can do. "Yes, I can drive to ballet and supervise the pre-ballet group." "Sure—I can make costumes for the play." "Yes, I'll serve at the dinner." "Sell tickets to the musical? Sure, why not?" When we say yes, we need to look inside ourselves and see what's motivating us. "Inside every woman who's compelled to perform lies a gnawing sense of inferiority."[10]

When someone says to me, "I don't know how you do it all!" I need to ask myself, "Why do I need to do it all?" I may find it hard to say no, or I may find it easy to fill my life with "safe" chores when I am lacking in self-esteem. Sometimes women actually invite abuse. "Go ahead, walk all over me; that's all I'm worth."

So we hear these temptations, "Try this . . . then you'll feel great about yourself . . . then that loneliness in your heart will be quenched." We must recognize that our longing for self-esteem may lead us down countless dead-end streets—engaging in unhealthy relationships, searching for acclaim in frantic volunteer work, seeking attention with newer and niftier designer clothes, manipulating children toward perfection. None of these endeavors fill the gaping hole at the center of our lives.

In fact the gaping hole gets only bigger. The lack of self-esteem, which is the flip side of pride, tears us apart to make room for other deadly sins: greed, gluttony, laziness, anger, lust and envy. Unhappy, because we have not given God center stage in our lives, we have substituted something else for God.

Jesus and Temptation

The Samaritan woman at the well knew she was worthless: she was a woman, she was a Samaritan, she was a social outcast because of her sexual practices. This woman had so little sense of self-esteem that she was stunned when Jesus spoke to her. Amazed, she asked him, "How is it that you, a Jew, ask a drink of me, a woman of Samaria?" This woman had spent years trying to fill her life with a stream of male relationships, always hoping that one would make her feel good about who she was. Who knows how many men she might have tried by the end of her lifetime, if she hadn't met Jesus?

How did Jesus respond to this woman? He saw her multiple sexual sins as indications of a deeper need that could be met only through coming to know him as Messiah. "Everyone who drinks of this water will be thirsty again, but those who drink of the water that I will give them will never be thirsty. The water that I will give will become in them a spring of water gushing up to eternal life" (Jn 4:13-14). Jesus didn't ignore her sin; he helped her name and own it. (That's what Part II of this book is all about.) But Jesus recognized that her sin, as heinous as it was, was simply not as important as this woman's deep-seated need to know God at the center of her life. (That's Part III.)

Jesus knew that when the Samaritan woman's deep needs were met, she might still be tempted. But he also knew that this woman's life would begin to be changed, in radical and wonderful ways. Jesus expected a lot from her. He expected more than a few isolated incidents of good behavior as a result of his encounter with this woman: he seemed to expect that she would begin to build a new life.

PART II
SYMPTOMS:
TRYING TO FILL THE
ACHING GAP

3/TRUSTING EXTERNALS TO MAKE US FEEL GOOD

*T*hree fourteen-year-old girls stand by the lake. They push their hair back and bend over their lighters, nonchalantly lighting their cigarettes. They inhale deeply and blow the smoke up, trying desperately to look nineteen. They strut a few steps as if they are being filmed, though I am the only person watching them. I am struck by the deathly importance of their appearance, and not just their looks. These girls care more than anything about how they measure up to some mysterious standard of coolness. It's more important than disobeying their parents, enjoying a lovely evening, jeopardizing their future health. I want to shake them and say, "Listen . . . it doesn't matter that much what other people think of you. Just be yourselves. You're jeopardizing your health and future." I don't, of course. They would look at me and at each other, "Hey, chill out, lady." They wouldn't understand what I was saying, and besides, who am I to talk?

Eager to Please

That desperate urge to impress strikes us as pathetic in young teens, but we all know it in our own lives. I certainly know it in myself. Men, but also women, seem to feel the need to prove themselves to each other. Why and how women display pride may differ from their male counterparts, but the sin is just as deadly. It is the root of all other sins because it keeps us from God. Gerald Hughes said, "Pride is when we want all creation to praise, reverence and honor us rather than God."[1] The proud, according to the Bible, will be judged because they exalt themselves (Is 2:12), they boast in themselves and not God (Jer 9:23, Gal 6:4) and they don't associate with the lowly (Rom 12:16).

I want everyone to think that I'm wonderful—a great cook, a profound thinker, a terrific writer, an outstanding teacher, a subtle wit, an extraordinary athlete for my age. A few years ago I realized that I was pressuring myself, so I started a program to be more human. If I am standing in a checkout line and hear a woman in the next line saying, "See if I ever bring you here again, you little brat," I say, "I'm sometimes like that with my kids." Or when I'm introducing myself in September to new classes: "And I have three children, and boy am I glad they're back in school. Much as I love them, by the end of summer we're about ready to finish each other off." Pretty humble.

But deep inside, I still want everyone to think I'm wonderful. I see this in myself when I'm tempted to exaggerate or lie to show myself in a better light. "I tried to phone you a couple of times." (Well, maybe only once.) "We almost never eat red meat anymore." (Though I guess we had it twice last week.) "If he had said that to me, I would have told him." (I probably would have sat seething in silence.) When I find an exaggeration or untruth on the tip of my tongue, it is because I want to prove to someone how extraordinary I am. Why in the world do I need to do that?

Displaying Trophies at the Center of Our Lives

The temptation to pride, the temptation to rely on externals to make me feel good about myself, is not the same as genuinely feeling good about myself or about a job well done. In fact, it may be the opposite. Trying to heap up trophies to prove how worthwhile I am springs from a poor self-image. I believe that I am not loved and accepted so I desperately try to fill in the blank with external successes.

If we as women tend to have low self-esteem, then our desire to use externals to bolster sagging self-images is understandable. That bolstering may come in any number of ways: surrounding ourselves with things, trying to have the perfect body, or reaching for professional success. Thirty years ago we might have tried to find our trophies exclusively in our homes and families; now we can find them in the workplace as well. Wherever we find them, these trophies will not bring satisfaction within.

Three years ago I went to a retreat center to spend a day in prayer, Bible reading and listening to God. The Lord spoke to me about pride. I realized how heavily I was relying on externals to bolster my self-esteem and how very important it was to me that people think I'm good. The articles I'd published, my doctoral work, my outstanding children, my lovely house, all these externals would make me worthy somehow.

But as long as I was clutching these accomplishments, I could not reach to God with open hands. I understood why James wrote, "God opposes the proud, but gives grace to the humble" (Jas 4:6, cf. 1 Pet 5:5-6). He can only give grace to those who aren't trying to prove how wonderful they are. I asked for God's forgiveness and prayed that he would continue to show me when I'm tempted to rely on externals. As I have struggled with pride over the last few years, I've realized how deep the root of this temptation goes. My need to impress goes back into my early childhood.

I was a middle child. My older brother was nearly five years older than I was, and I understood when I was very young that I could never hope to match his precocious mischief. My younger brother was eighteen months younger than I; he would always be the adorable baby. I was left with the role of the good child. If I was good and sweet, then adults (the most important people) would think I was worthy.

One Christmas morning when I was four, we all gathered around the tree. My great-aunt Edie said, "Can little Mary Ellen open this package first?" I took the box and unwrapped it. Inside was a doll with black wavy hair and dark, brown-painted eyes. A bride's dress, a yellow chiffon prom dress and a red square dance dress were in the box. "You know, Mary Ellen," my mother said. "this is a very special doll, to be looked after carefully, like a big girl." I jumped up and kissed Edie.

My older brother was given a package to open and the spotlight shifted to him. I picked up the doll and moved to my bedroom. I knelt on the floor, cradling her in my arms, waiting. I knew it wouldn't take long for them to miss me, to come and find me in this endearing position. They would think I was a delightful child.

I heard my father in the doorway, speaking in his stage

whisper. "Grace, Edie, come and look here." I held my pose while Mom's footsteps and Edie's shuffle got to the doorway. "Isn't that cute?" Mom said.

"I guess she does like it. I thought she would but you never know," Edie added.

Four years later I was still striving for external recognition. I pushed open the door and put my books on the table. "Mom? You home?" No answer. I pulled open the flap on the manila envelope and let the report card slide onto the table. All *A's* except one *B+* in math.

My stomach felt cold and tight. I didn't want a *B+*. I conjured an image of my mother saying, "Wonderful job, Mary Ellen. All *A's*." My big brother didn't get all *A's*.

I found a pencil and started erasing the *B*. The blotch got bigger, darker and smudgier. Over the blotch, I penned an *A*.

I heard the car in the driveway and slipped the card into the envelope. I wiped the pink and smudgy eraser dust onto the floor. "Hi, Mom. My report card is here, but I thought I'd wait till you got home to open it." Of course she realized that someone had been erasing the grade. Wisely, she didn't punish me. But why was I so desperate to excel?

I don't remember being pushed to perform or pressured to be endearing or academically excellent, and yet somehow I thought that external success would make me feel important and good.

"What do you do?" That can be a dreadful question for women. By the time I had my encounter with pride three years ago, the what-do-you-do question wasn't so bad for me. For years I had to answer, "Oh, I'm home with the kids." Now I could say off-handedly, "Oh, I'm a writer, and I teach writing to college students, and I'm in a Ph.D. program." It sounded great, almost as if I were saying, "Yes, I'm smart, and creative and high-energy." These are all externals that the world rewards and respects. After my retreat day I realized that my answer to *the question* only meant that I was trying harder. In fact, I knew I was no more important or better than my friend Joan. She doesn't have a terrific answer to *the question,* but she loves people and cares for them by giving them her time.

When I put external successes in the center of my life, I have come to believe what our culture tells women is valuable about them. I lose God's perspective on who I am and what makes me lovable and worthy. I have swallowed the lies of the world where worth is measured in what we do rather than who we are.

Even if we haven't tried to find success in a job or school, we may transfer the urge for success to our families and demand that they perform well—to make us look good. I chatted with a couple at a family camp. The mother was finishing her medical degree and the father was a partner in a prestigious local law firm. I asked the father what their teenage daughter was doing. He answered me, pride glowing in his eyes as he put his arm across her shoulders, "Jackie is finishing up her vo-tech training, and she'll be a cafeteria worker, won't you honey?" She beamed and the mother squeezed her hand.

What's so extraordinary about this scene? Most of us want our children to make us proud, and we often judge our children by the world's standards. We hope our children will give us something to brag about. When people's children are excelling in music, going off to Stanford, or winning a sports scholarship, we are more impressed than if they are happy and well adjusted. This couple seemed so pleased that their daughter was doing what she wanted to do, enjoying it. They were proud and happy though it didn't bolster their egos.

I've sometimes been guilty of transferring my need for external success to my children. When we make a fuss over our children's *A's,* their recitals, or their soccer victories, we imply that external successes impress us and make us proud. When I look back on my mothering, I see myself wanting my children to be as good as I am (or maybe a little more perfect, since I was giving them such a super-enriched upbringing).

We want our children to reflect well on us, just as Mrs. Zebedee's did. She'd raised those boys right. She knew she had outstanding sons who deserved to sit at Jesus' right and left hands. She wanted them to get their proper place and reflect well on her. The other disciples all started to grumble, and so we see in this story what we know from our own experience: pride alienates. When we focus on our external successes, others envy and resent us, withdrawing from us.

The Good Mother

As soon as my son Andrew was born, I knew that I needed to be the perfect mother. I had to breastfeed on demand, keep the house tidy, bake cookies and whole wheat bread, never discipline in anger, always be available to lend an ear to my husband's needs, never demand any time for myself, make my children avid readers by reading to them almost from birth, not miss out on any of their babyhood milestones, expose them to Brahms, make them appliqued dungarees, raise them to love goodness, help them identify a Crested Hoopoe.

As Andrew got older and Stephen arrived I spent hours seeking out enriching experiences for them. We visited shops looking for educational toys. We went on daily outings to the botanical gardens, the museum, the harbor, the bird sanctuary. We watched no television but read for hours. When Andrew was three we made our first trip of eight by now I think through *The Chronicles of Narnia.* I would drop a sewing project to run and see the steam train go past. When Andrew took a fifty-pound bag of flour and dumped it on the kitchen floor, I let him play with it for the afternoon, thinking it would be an educational experience.

If an external observer had been judging me, I might have received a "supermother award." But the evenings haunted me.

I would kiss Andrew good night and check on Stephen. I'd pick up baby Susannah who sucked and whimpered until she was asleep. I'd put her in her crib. Then I would go to the kitchen and make a cup of tea and sit in the living room. The sound of hymns being sung at the evening service across the street would waft through the evening air. I'd open *Pride and Prejudice* and start to read.

Suddenly I would remember. That morning I had yelled at Andrew when he took Stephen's train. Yelling wasn't even the word; I had bellowed at him, "Andrew, Stephen's trying to play a nice game; will you leave him alone!" Better go make it better. I would walk upstairs to his room. Andrew sprawled, looking like an angel, mouth open slightly. How could I have yelled at this child? He's so little, and he's jealous with a new baby in the house. What was I teaching him, yelling at him like that? I would kiss him gently, wishing the kiss could be like an indulgence that would pay off the day's misdeeds.

"Mother-guilt" is so common that it is part of being a mother. Harriet Lerner in *The Dance of Intimacy* says of this problem: "Feelings of guilt run deepest and are most ingrained in mothers, who are the first to be blamed, the first to blame themselves." She points out that guilt is not an individual problem because our society "assigns mothers the primary responsibility for all family problems, excuses men from real fathering and provides remarkably little support for the actual needs of children and families. A mother is encouraged to believe she is her child's environment, and that if only she is a 'good enough' mother, her children will flourish."[2]

We can never be good enough as mothers to satisfy ourselves or our society. And it's not even clear that Jesus puts our being wonderful mothers as the greatest priority. When someone told Jesus that his mother and brothers were standing outside, Jesus replied, "Whoever does the will of my Father in heaven is my brother and sister and mother" (Mt 12:50).

I was fortunate. My daughter refused to cooperate with my desire to enlist her as the third perfect child in a perfect family. I assumed that Susannah would allow me to enrich her life. She refused. She wouldn't be me, or belong to me; she wanted to be herself.

When Susannah was born, her body followed her dark, curly head, and the doctor shouted, "A girl!" I cried. For several weeks each time I realized I had a girl, tears formed in my eyes. Here was a girl-child, one with whom I could share my life. We could be friends and maybe grow flowers together and cook and knit.

I hugged her infant body. But she screamed and twisted and pulled from me. She was restless and didn't thrive; she didn't want to breastfeed. By the time she was seven months old, she would only nurse if I woke her at ten o'clock and let her suck when she was too dozy to fight.

Susannah weaned herself at nine months and threw away her pacifier a month or two later. She didn't want to be dependent on anything. Her brothers were quiet readers. Susannah woke at five-thirty on Saturdays singing at the top of her lungs. She told people exactly what she thought of their clothes, cars, opinions and habits. Susannah told smokers that they should quit; she asked friends whom I was gently evangelizing, "Why don't you go to church? Aren't you a Christian? Why not?"

I learned from Susannah that the three children for whom

I am responsible are not mine. They are ultimately God's, and they are also their own. They were not entrusted to my care to reflect well on me. I need to be careful whenever I link who I am with their external successes or failures.

Sarah wanted to have a perfect son so that God could fulfill his promises to herself and Abraham. She decided to help God out and offered her maid Hagar to Abraham. Her motives were probably good—"God seems to be having trouble managing this situation so I'll give him a hand. I can control things, thank you." But the results of her urge to control were disastrous. And I think that our urge to control our children can be disastrous. Either willingly or unwillingly we have to give up the myth that external success will fulfill our lives and that we can control our lives to make ourselves look pretty good.

Finding a New Perspective
No matter what the external success, it never satisfies. Nothing external can fill that gap for a woman wondering whether she is worthy. A friend of mine does free-lance editing for some of the big publishing houses. She said to me the other day, "If I haven't gotten a manuscript from Harper & Row in two weeks, I totally lose my confidence. I assume that I've made a terrible mistake on a manuscript or that they've decided that they never want to give me work again. Why does this feeling never go away?" External successes will never satisfy us. If we don't realize this, we will try to control our family and our world; we will feel that we are the ones who have to make everything work.

We long for success. It is my experience and the experience of many others that external successes and goals simply do not work to fill that space. When I am most excited about an article's success or the way something goes right for a child, the next day I am casting around for the next success to fill the gap. Only Jesus can fill that gap.

To begin to deal with pride, I need to look carefully at the external successes I depend on. Do I find myself trying to impress new people when I meet them with how important or interesting or wonderful I am? Do I think a lot about the impression I am making, wondering what other people think of me? Do I think that *if only* I got a particular job or my child had a particular success, then I would feel good and fulfilled? Have I believed that I am not worthwhile unless I have certain degrees and successes with family or career? Am I trying to surround myself with external successes to achieve a security that is not possible outside of God?

If I find myself too concerned with what the world rates as important achievements, I may be listening to the wrong voices. Roman Catholic writer Henri Nouwen suggests that often our "productivity"—our many activities and successes—is in fact a desperate urge to escape a sense of sterility.[3] I am substituting "what I do" for God; I am putting my doctoral hood, clipped-out magazine articles and pictures of the kids at the center of my life and saying, "These are what make me important."

Although I believe it is crucial that women use their gifts, stretch their minds, expand their horizons, they cannot look for fulfillment from accumulated external successes. Paul suggests to the believers in Galatia that they must be responsible stewards of their gifts: "All must test their own work; then that work, rather than their neighbor's work, will become a cause for pride. For all must carry their own loads" (Gal 6:4). Our gifts are from God. Not ours to own. We hold them with open hands. Sometimes those around us can help us keep God's perspective on our external successes. They may encourage us to stretch ourselves into new areas, pull us back up when we fail and help us see that who we are, not what we do, is important.

We need more and more to find our security and fulfillment in our relationship to Christ. We need to enjoy our successes without relying on them too heavily. I need to practice saying to myself, "Well, I'm happy that this is going to be published; I knew it was a pretty good article, but it's not the whole world to me. I am who I am, loved and worthy, not because of this article or other things I do but simply because God loves me."

The areas that the world calls success may not be the ones that God sees as truly important. The disciples wanted to send children away from their busy, important Master, but Jesus welcomed them and saw them as important. The poor, the politically disenfranchised, they were the ones to whom Jesus gave his time and attention.

When Hannah presented Samuel to the Lord, she prayed: "There is no Holy One like the Lord, no one besides you; there is no Rock like our God. Talk no more so very proudly, let not arrogance come from your mouth; for the Lord is a God of knowledge, and by him actions are weighed" (1 Sam 2:2-3).

Jesus is our example. He had all the glory of heaven but set it aside for a womb, a manger, a life of costly ministry and death on a cross. Paul instructed the Christians at Philippi to follow his example: "Let the same mind be in you that was in Christ Jesus, who, though he was in the form of God, did not regard equality with God as something to be exploited, but emptied himself, taking the form of a slave, being born in human likeness. And being found in human form, he humbled himself and became obedient to the point of death—even death on a cross" (Phil 2:5-8).

When Jesus washed the disciples' feet, he was deliberately flouting the worldly hierarchy that gives the job of footwashing to those who "don't count": "So if I, your Lord and Teacher, have washed your feet, you also ought to wash one another's feet" (Jn 13:14).

I met Arne one night at a dinner party. I felt particularly clever that night; my jokes and puns seemed awfully cute to me, and everyone laughed at them. I talked about my writing, my studies, and Arne sat on his chair and smiled. He pulled out my chair at the dinner table, which seemed sort of old-fashioned and sweet. The jokes and political discussions seemed to whirl around him; he enjoyed his meal and smiled.

Later as we sipped coffee in the living room, Arne's wife told us his story. He had been a teacher for many years. One autumn evening he was riding his bicycle home from the library when a car stopped suddenly in front of him. He hit the car and was thrown over it. Arne's helmet slipped off, and he landed on his head. Arne was in a coma for twenty-eight days. The family despaired. Then one day he opened his eyes and began to look at them. The accident had occurred six years ago, his wife told me.

We sat in silence after the story. Then Arne spoke, "I'm not as sharp as I was . . . it takes me awhile to get things . . . but I have much deeper feelings, deeper empathy for people. I think I love people more deeply."

I listened to him and thought about how vastly more important compassion and empathy are than cleverness in God's eyes. Then Arne spoke again: "God moves in a mysterious way," he said.

We need God's help to gain a new perspective on what is important in our lives. We need to find ourselves in God, not in our accomplishments.

4/FILLING OUR LIVES
WITH THINGS

I *throw a tennis ball along the grassy riverbank for our golden* retriever. Caddie gallops joyfully after it and drops it at my feet. She twitches with expectation until I throw it again. My son, Stephen, pulls another tennis ball out of his pocket and hands it to Caddie. She tries to pick it up and loses the other ball. She tries to fit both balls in her mouth, but one rolls away. She drops one and picks up the other, back and forth, so busy holding onto her possessions that she has forgotten the joy of galloping along the river on a June day.

Like Caddie, I am tempted to accumulate things and give them all my attention. I see a navy corduroy skirt in a catalogue and that skirt keeps popping into my mind—how nice it would look and how useful for when I teach! I fantasize about redoing our upper floor into a bedroom suite with skylights. Working at the school rummage sale I find myself thinking, "This lamp is awfully nice . . . and what a bargain!"

Greed: The Temptation

The earliest folk tales tell of greed (Ali Baba and the Forty Thieves, Rumpelstiltskin, and so on), but I suspect the desire to fill our lives with things is more pervasive in the late twentieth century. In our society greed is assumed, even promoted; greed is literally at the heart of our consumer society. Companies spend millions on advertisements that skillfully press our buttons: "Of course I deserve a little treat!" "Well, Jan has one and think how much she has used it; I deserve one, too." We forget that greed is sin.

Jesus took greed very seriously, and he talked more about money than he did about resurrection or judgment. Jesus understood human nature and realized that money and possessions would pull us away from God. "Take care!" Jesus said. "Be on your guard against all kinds of greed; for one's life does not consist in the abundance of possessions" (Lk 12:15). We agree with Jesus; we know that money isn't everything. But our culture intones to us another message: "Of course your life consists of what you have. You don't have a boat? Poor thing. You don't own a home? You really ought to. Remember, the one who dies with the most toys wins."

We hear this message over and over, sometimes subtly, sometimes blatantly, and we begin to forget that things don't bring us satisfaction; we forget that God did not create us to find satisfaction in things. The thought—we really need that new couch—sneaks in and begins to prey on our minds. We mull it over and then go out looking for one. We finally find just the right one, and the shop assistant assures us that we are in luck. There's a special short-term deal that would give us a chair to match the couch for only an extra $250. We order them. We wait two weeks, practically breathless, for the new couch and chair to arrive. Every time we pass through the living room, we wonder how in the world we have been able to stand that ripped old thing so long. Finally the great day arrives and the movers bring in the couch and chair. It looks even better than we thought!

But the elation lasts only a day or two. Why? Because things never satisfy.

We think that the reason the new couch and chair haven't brought ultimate satisfaction is how despicable the carpet looks. The living room will look gorgeous when we get a new carpet; then we will really feel satisfied. The world tells us that we will find satisfaction in things.

We are tempted to fill our lives with things because we are surrounded by the world's messages all the time. But these messages find resonance in ourselves, our flesh. The urge to satisfy ourselves with a new dress, car, chair, bowl, or plant seems fresh to us every time. The new thing we get (whatever it is) never satisfies, so we are always vulnerable to the next temptation. Notice that our cunning enemy doesn't remind us that our last purchase didn't satisfy. We aren't told, "Well, maybe that new couch didn't satisfy you, but certainly the carpet will!" Satan's message is more subtle, often simply the image of the thing—the pretty blouse, the lawn chair on an idyllic summer afternoon, luring us to indulge.

Our society accepts and promotes greed. The message that the world has so successfully marketed has crept into the church. Making heaps of money and driving BMW's are the ideals of many of today's university students. What may be surprising (or maybe not) is that these ideals are equally accepted in Christian colleges.

The church (or the Christian college) often speaks out strongly against immorality but overlooks greed and covetousness. What would Jesus have said to the way the rich are often put on church and college boards of trustees, as if they were somehow more important than the poor?

Greed is not a problem only because it twists our values; it also wastes time. Promoting God's kingdom takes a back seat because our time and money go for new hardwood floors, the deck we've always wanted, or a new car. People become less important because spending hours by the bedside of a terminally ill patient doesn't help our bottom line. As the spirit of the world infects our thinking, earning money is all that counts.

The apostle Paul warned growing churches: "But fornication and impurity of any kind, or greed, must not even be mentioned among you. . . . Be sure of this, that no fornicator or impure person, or one who is greedy (that is, an idolater), has any inheritance in the kingdom of Christ and of God" (Eph 5:3, 5). We think we're okay because we're only doing what the rest of society does. We face a choice: love and worship God, or love and worship mammon.[1]

Greed: The Religion (or, Shop Till You Drop)

I passed an outlet mall on the Pennsylvania Turnpike. A huge sign read: "Eat, Sleep and Shop." What else, indeed, would a person really want to do in life? Scores of tour buses lined the parking lot.

In our society we may parrot "In God We Trust"; but the reality is "In Things We Trust." That's how we live. A society that has lost a genuine belief in God doesn't become godless;

it designs other gods for itself. In a society that no longer really believes in God, materialism becomes our religion. When Jesus talked about mammon, he wasn't discussing just money but anything that becomes a god in our lives (Mt 6:24; Lk 16:13). Paul told the Christians at Colossae that greed is idolatry (Col 3:5) because it places something in the center of our lives that doesn't belong there.

Shopping is the worship and sacrament of the religion materialism. Shopping was not always a national pastime and a recreational activity. Think back to Laura Ingalls Wilder's *Little House in the Big Woods.* Remember Laura's first trip to town with the family when they went into the General Goods Shop? They traded furs and bought some tea "and a little paper package of store sugar to have in the house when company came."[2] Then they picked out several yards of fabric for two new shirts for Pa, some cloth for new sheets and underwear. They were overwhelmed when the storekeeper gave them each a piece of candy. Shopping was a necessity that was carried on several times a year in order to get supplies that were needed and maybe an occasional treat. Not so in twentieth-century America. Shopping is a recreational activity, and guess who is happiest about that? The retailers who make big bucks, the credit card companies who make loads of money on interest as shoppers overextend themselves buying things they don't need.

Greed: The Realization of the Sickness

Judy, a thirty-six-year-old attorney, took several years to realize that things didn't satisfy and that her greed was threatening to wreck her life. She called herself a shopping addict.

After her divorce Judy had very little money; she made all her own clothes as she supported herself and her son and went to law school. Then she joined a lucrative law practice and married a man whose business had started to take off. She started shopping for professional clothes, but the big change came when she went to Europe on business.

In Europe Judy met a woman who was "classy." Judy had seen wealthy women spending heaps of money in American stores on clothes, but this woman was different. She used her creative ability to choose lovely fabrics and stunning outfits. Judy came back from France and Portugal with the specific goal of dressing like that woman. She didn't want closets full of clothes; she didn't want name-brand or even high-fashion stuff, but she wanted to look classy.

Gradually Judy's buying got out of hand. She found that once she started buying good quality clothes, she didn't want cheap stuff. She told herself that she had two lifestyles to dress for: one as a wife and mom, the other as a professional. She told herself that she was buying things she really loved, not clothes that would sit in her closet. She prided herself on the fact that she wore her clothes to death. And, of course, she could always find people who were worse than she. She had heard about Donald Trump's excesses and Imelda Marcos's thousands of shoes. She read articles about people whose shopping ruined them, like the woman whom journalist Kim Wright Wiley describes. This woman earned $70,000 a year but got herself financially overextended to the point where she set the thermostat in her condo so low that her pipes froze.[3]

Sometimes Judy felt uncomfortable. She found herself using the word *need* and wondering what it meant. "I need some emerald green shoes to match that new jacket," or "I need a red coat for those in-between autumn days." She began to feel that she couldn't go places without wearing a beautiful outfit. One day Judy figured out how much money she had spent during the last year on various luxuries and was appalled to find how much she had spent on clothes.

The crowning blow came when she went shopping one day and brought home a skirt, top, scarf and belt on which she'd spent over seven hundred dollars. "I got home and was literally sick to my stomach," Judy said. "I began to realize that shopping and clothes had got such a strong hold on me that it was frightening. I thought of people starving when I was spending this kind of money on clothes." Judy realized that her shopping was an evil thing that she needed to deal with and get control of.

Why Have We Bought the World's Line?

Greed is a problem because of what we have been told by our culture, because of what has seeped into the church. I wonder if there are any people living in the Western world who don't find greed nagging at their lives. Women are the ones who have been caricatured as the serious shoppers. Perhaps, with our associations with the home and family, we usually have been responsible for material goods. After all, if I don't buy new underpants for the ten-year-old, no one else will. But if we look closely at our shopping habits we see something else. We find ourselves investing too much energy and emotion in our clothing, hobby buying and home decorating. Once again we try to fill the need at our center with something that leaves it more empty than before.

Why have women bought into these lies? Perhaps women struggle with spending as a "reward-punishment" syndrome, not unlike certain eating disorders.[4] A woman feels rejected and goes shopping for a new pair of shoes. Buying, writes Collette Dowling (author of several popular books on women's psychology), "compensates us for deep-seated feelings of being without, of being 'not enough' within ourselves. . . . Buying, says a male friend of mine, is an act of female macho. That, or it's an

act of female desperation. We consume in order to feel strong.
We consume in order not to feel eaten alive by our own dep-
rivation."[5]

Greed: The Illusion of Control

Lovely fabrics, a pottery collection, a welcoming home: there is
nothing inherently wrong with these things. For many of us
home decorating is a rare creative outlet; the problem is the
place that we give it in our lives. When we use the new outfit
to make us feel better, or we believe that the newer, bigger
house will bring us satisfaction, or we swallow the line that the
new washing machine or car will put us in control of our life,
then we are buying into the world's lies and ignoring Paul's
words to Timothy: "But those who want to be rich fall into
temptation and are trapped by many senseless and harmful
desires that plunge people into ruin and destruction. For the
love of money is a root of all kinds of evil, and in their eager-
ness to be rich some have wandered away from the faith and
pierced themselves with many pains" (1 Tim 6:9-10).

The illusion—"if only I had a new outfit, a new couch, a new
kitchen"—speaks to us of the fact that God is not central in our
lives. When God is central in our lives we will believe the counsel of Jesus, "Therefore I tell you, do not worry about your life,
what you will eat or what you will drink, or about your body,
what you will wear. Is not life more than food, and the body
more than clothing?" (Mt 6:25).

When we attempt to use things to fill the gaping hole inside
us, it's time to look carefully at our lives, to ask what this desperate desire means about our level of security with God.
Clothes, home furnishings, electronics: even if they're not bad
in themselves, they feed our human desire to be in control of
our lives.

When I knew that we would be moving from our lovely old rectory in Cape Town, before I even had any idea which continent we would live on, let alone what kind of house, I began decorating our home-to-be. I pored over *Better Homes and Gardens* and *Ladies Home Journal* looking for money-saving ideas such as using wicker in a living room and open shelves rather than cabinets in a kitchen. I bought baskets at craft fairs and imagined them clustered at the end of a raised hearth in front of a crackling fire.

I also began drawing, sketching floor plans, with furniture placed carefully. I asked myself, "Would the teak tallboy look better in the living room or dining room?" "Wouldn't it be nice to get some African Yellowwood furniture while we are in a position to buy it?" I sketched and resketched, shopped at auctions and antique shops, tracked down curtain sales at the Golden Acre Shopping Mall.

I told myself that I was simply eager to make a home for my family, a nest for the children, a wonderful place for my weary husband to relax. It sure sounded Christian to me. One day I was reading Matthew 8 and came across the part where Jesus says, "Foxes have holes, and birds of the air have nests; but the Son of Man has nowhere to lay his head" (v. 20). I was stunned that Jesus could say something that seemed so contrary to the books I'd read on the Christian homemaker. I'd got the impression that surrounding myself and my family with creature comforts and beautiful objects was a godly activity.

I began wondering why I was sketching and shopping, why I had a feeling that I had to get over to that store while their sale was still on. I realized that I was looking for security in things. If I bought a lamp, it was a physical thing that I could touch and look at, and that lamp would one day be switched on somewhere even if I didn't now know which continent it would be on. It made me feel a whole lot better. It made me feel as if I was in control.

I still see this in myself. Recently when I was asked to speak at a large conference, I was nervous because the audience might not be particularly keen on my insights as a Christian who teaches writing. Two days before my flight, I knew I had to go to a classy women's store and find a new outfit. Something stunning. Then I'd feel okay. Maybe a new haircut would help. I even thought of replacing my contact lenses.

When that desire to shop emerges, when I start feeling nagged from within—"Justers is still open, you could just pop in"—then I know it's time for me to look inside and see why I am so desperate for some new thing.

The Illusion That Ownership Brings Control

I want to control my life; one way I seek to do this is by owning things. I want to know they're mine. Every summer we have three weeks on an island in Puget Sound where my parents own a cabin. The weather is lovely and cool, the water shimmers blue, the children poke along the beach, kingfishers flash overhead. It is perfect. But my husband and I find as we walk and talk that we look at the houses with their lovely views built on spectacular lots, and we begin to wish that we owned one. We talk about what we would do if we suddenly had some money and which property we'd buy. We become discontented and greedy. Here we are in this wonderful place, but we're not happy to use a cabin. We want to own a piece of this island. We want to control our future so that we can always spend our summers there.

Our best reality check is to walk to the local luxury resort, where people moor their 100-foot yachts (some complete with a helicopter landing pad on deck), their 70-foot schooners, their seaplanes. People strut their designer clothes and designer tans and talk about which restaurant has the finest fresh salmon, the best Cabernet Sauvignon for dinner. We sit on a bench and look at them. Their eyes are empty; they snap at each other. If the weather is perfect, they don't notice. If the weather is not perfect, they grump. They are like children whose naps are long overdue. Clearly, things do not bring satisfaction, and even ownership doesn't bring control.

Sadly, the look in their eyes is not unlike the look in many Christians' eyes, eyes that have bought the world's line and believe that satisfaction is to be found in comforts of various kinds, ownership of things around us. Most of us in the West are comfortable, even wealthy, by world standards. Maybe Jesus was right when he said, "It will be hard for a rich person to enter the kingdom of heaven" (Mt 19:23).

Why is it so hard for us rich and greedy Westerners to enter the kingdom of heaven? Because our things provide us with temporary satisfaction (and we seem unable to remember that the satisfaction conveyed by a new purchase is oh-so-fleeting). Our things give us an illusion of control. Paul wrote to Timothy: "As for those who in the present age are rich, command them not to be haughty, or to set their hopes on the uncertainty of riches, but rather on God who richly provides us with everything for our enjoyment" (1 Tim 6:17). We surround ourselves with comforts and things and begin to believe that we control our own lives.

Denise's Story

Denise and her husband John moved to Australia from a small town in England. They wanted a bigger house and to give their two-year-old son Matthew some of the opportunities they had never had. My husband, Ernie, and I saw them off at London's

Heathrow airport in 1974, a few months before we were married. For a couple of years we heard from them only occasionally: "John's working days, and I'm working nights, so we can get together the down payment on a house. We've found an area near the beach that we like. I bought a dryer last week, and we've set aside a master bedroom set that is beautiful. The weather has been great. . . ."

One summer evening in Cape Town, Ernie brought home a letter from Denise. We sat and read together. She explained that Matthew had a very rare form of cancer and that he wasn't expected to live very long. From the time he was four until he died at age seven, we heard occasionally from her, telling us about the course of the cancer, the treatments. We also heard that a church near their home had befriended them and was caring for them in their pain. Several years after Matthew died, Denise gave birth to twin sons. The church helped her care for them.

Last summer Denise visited. We hadn't seen her in fifteen years, and we knew that many things in her life had changed. She had become a Christian; she had lost a child and now had twins. We knew she'd be different but we were unprepared for her total transformation. Fifteen years older, she is radiant, lovely. She works with handicapped children, which doesn't pay very well, but she loves them and finds great satisfaction in bringing joy to their lives.

After several days of marveling at her transformation, I asked her how the experience of Matthew's death had affected her.

"I realized how totally unimportant things are," she said. "When you've got a sick child and you would give anything you've got or could ever, ever buy to have the child well . . . then you see how unimportant things are.

"I also realized," she said, "that buying things had given me a sense of control. As long as I could buy things, decorate a home, have a new car, I felt that I was in control of my life. Of course none of us are really in control. I guess I've finally realized that."

The control we strive for with our purchases is an illusion. After telling his followers the story of the rich fool, Jesus went on, "Do not be afraid, little flock, for it is your Father's good pleasure to give you the kingdom. Sell your possessions, and give alms. Make purses for yourselves that do not wear out, an unfailing treasure in heaven, where no thief comes near and no moth destroys. For where your treasure is, there your heart will be also" (Lk 12:32-34).

The Opposites of Greed: Contentment and Generosity

Paul wrote to Timothy: "Of course, there is great gain in godliness combined with contentment; for we brought nothing into the world, so that we can take nothing out of it; but if we have food and clothing, we will be content with these" (1 Tim 6:6). Contentment and satisfaction are the great enemies of a consumer society, of advertising, of greed.

To build contentment, we must look at our greed and see what it is telling us about ourselves. Am I being honest about greed in my life, or do I justify things as needs when they're not? Do I spend more money than I should on non-necessities? Do I think that things will bring me satisfaction if only I could own them? Have I believed some of the lies about women needing to shop to be happy? Have I believed that I am not worthwhile unless I have great clothes or own and decorate my home beautifully? Am I trying to surround myself with things to achieve a security that is not possible outside of God?

To build contentment we also need to remember that what our greed tells us is a lie. We need to be ready to answer the lie: "Ha! Do you expect me to believe that a new outfit will make me a new, confident person? Even though it's never worked in the past! Do you expect me to believe that having a new dining room table is going to make me contented? Ha! If I buy a crock pot, I'll have to find cupboard space for it; if we move I'll have to move it. The picture of it in the advertisement doesn't show the crock pot languishing in a bottom cupboard with the wok, the rice steamer and heaven knows what else! I don't need this thing! Why should I let it clutter my life?"

If we find it hard to shout louder than society and the media, then it helps to be accountable to someone. If a purchase is over thirty dollars, my husband and I have a policy that we don't succumb to even the most exciting bargain without waiting forty-eight hours and discussing it. We rely on each other for perspective.

Paul urges Christians to be content with what they have, and we can encourage ourselves to "not be led into temptation" by some of our choices. For many of us poring over catalogues or shopping when we don't need specific things is like flipping through a *Playboy* magazine; it is our effort to "lead ourselves into temptation." We see all the things that we don't have; we begin to think that we deserve them. We can avoid shopping unless we need something specific and use a list when we must shop.

Here's an important principle: if a person doesn't shop, she doesn't buy things. Sounds silly; but when I find that I'm too busy to go to a mall or discount store, my bank statement lists far fewer checks written for unnecessary items. Shopping at garage sales or other sales can seem like good stewardship, but we probably accumulate more than we need. How many of us have basements (or attics or closets) that contain our bargains? Shopping itself promotes self-absorption; we think of ourselves, our needs and wants. Even Christmas shopping, supposedly for others, consists of thinking about what others will think of us if we get them this sweater and of how it compares in value to the present they got us last year.

To aim for contentment, then, we need to look at all we have and avoid exposure to forces that tell us we need more. If I say to myself, "I've got plenty of clothes, far more than most people in the world, and I cannot usefully use any more," then I should take the mail-order catalogues and throw them into the recycling bin without a glance. We can also avoid advertising, which is designed to undermine our contentment and encourage our greed. If I start to look through the ads I begin to think, "Hey, that's a cute blouse. Wouldn't that look nice with my new skirt? And what a deal; I could save forty percent!" If I listen to advertisements on TV, I begin to think that we "need" one of the new mulching lawn-mowers. Advertising, and in fact our whole economy, is based on keeping people in a state of mind where they can never be satisfied—because the contented person is not vulnerable to a sales pitch. Our Enemy wants us to be fundamentally (and eternally) dissatisfied.

Part of contentment is perspective. We can choose whom we will compare ourselves with. When we are around wealthy friends I find myself thinking, "Boy, I'd like a cabin like this. Why can't we take a trip to Europe while the kids are still at an age to enjoy it? Poor old me!" I need to remind myself to think of friends who struggle to buy clothes for their children, to pay rent. Or how exorbitantly wealthy we are compared to the truly poor in much of the Third World. If we are properly involved with our poorer neighbors, helping in literacy programs, food pantries, or whatever, we will have a clearer perspective.

The other way to grow in our contentment is by giving. Generosity is the opposite of greed. I knew a family in Cape

Town who went through all their possessions yearly and took out anything that they hadn't used since the last sort-out. (This gives us perspective on our stuff.) And then they did something defiant and radical; they did not hold a garage sale but gave their things away. Richard Foster talks about the great response when greed raises its ugly head in our lives—give.[6] If we find that we are feeling too attached to some possession, we can give it away. Giving shatters our sense that what we have is our own. Generosity flows out, greed pulls in.

Freedom from greed is often evident in the generosity of Third World Christians. I learned my most important lesson about greed from Lizzy.

When we lived in South Africa I had a friend named Lizzy who was black and very poor. She earned a pittance to support herself and her two children by cleaning houses—day in, day out—with forty-pound Nzuzo strapped to her back. In her poverty she walked miles to save train fare.

A woman for whom Lizzy worked gave her a brand-new outfit for Nzuzo, from one of the nicest stores in town, a store that had a very liberal return policy. The outfit was too small for Nzuzo.

Lizzy came to me. "Mary Ellen, I want you to have this for Stephen."

"Lizzy, you could exchange this for another nice outfit that Nzuzo could wear."

"I know I could," she answered. "But my heart wants to give it to you. I want to see Stephen wear it."

"But Lizzy . . . an outfit like this is so expensive. Think carefully; you should exchange it."

"I know I could exchange it," she said patiently, "but what is money compared to love? I want to give it to you."

Sneaking into my consciousness was the realization that for

all my generosity (after all, hadn't I chosen to live in Africa?), money dominated my thinking and values.

Lizzy saw money in its proper perspective. Jesus recognized that we would be tempted to use money and possessions to find temporary satisfaction, control and a sense of self-worth. Jesus encourages his followers to invest, instead, in the treasure at the heart of our lives.

5/FOCUSING ON FOOD

Many of us eat too much, think about food more than we want to and spend too much money on food. We are tempted by wonderful Swiss chocolates at the cash register, raspberry truffles and Jamoca pecan fudge ice cream in the new shopping area, and sushi bars and Afghan delis clustered downtown. Food is pushed at us all the time: junk food, gourmet food, health and special diet food. Restaurants promote special "all you can eat" evenings and cruises provide three or four gorging sessions a day. Visitors to the United States are amazed at how much people here talk about food, how they even talk about the next meal (or a past memorable meal) as they eat their present meal and how much social life is centered on eating out. Food looms out of proportion; our focus is drawn from God to what our next meal will be, to the chocolate cake that beckons us from the kitchen.

We associate the deadly sin of gluttony with overeating, the debauched medieval banquet with sides of venison, whole roasted suckling pigs (complete with an apple in the mouth), pheasants and huge desserts as peasants stand longingly outside eating thin gruel. Or we think of the Roman banquets, people gorging themselves and then vomiting so that they could eat more. But gluttony as the temptation to overemphasize food is still alive and well in our society today.

The flesh is powerful in our lives: the stomach crying out for food, or perhaps worse yet, the chips in the kitchen shouting for attention! The dieter knows she shouldn't, knows she doesn't want to and yet she does, reminiscent of Paul's words in Romans 7: "I do not understand my own actions. For I do not do what I want, but I do the very thing I hate" (v. 15).

As a college roommate of mine used to put it (as she walked in the door with an ice-cream cake), "All we Christians do is eat. We can't drink, we can't smoke, we can't sleep around; so we eat."

The opposite of gluttony is self-disciplined eating. The self-disciplined eater recognizes food as a *gift from God* and *something to be shared.*

In the Old Testament food is seen as a gift from God that satisfies and even delights (Is 55:2). And food is meant to be shared with those in need. God requests his people to "share [their] bread with the hungry" (Is 58:7). A righteous person "gives . . . bread to the hungry" (Ezek 18:7).

In the New Testament Jesus told his followers not to be overly concerned with food because life is "more than food" (Mt

6:25). Jesus' flesh "is true food" (Jn 6:55). Like the children of Israel in the Old Testament, Christians are encouraged to be content if they have "food and clothing" (1 Tim 6:8) and to share with those in need (Jas 2:15). Our culture encourages discontent and stinginess, passing the plate for another helping as the poor starve. The results of gluttony—not being satisfied and not sharing—are only part of the story.

Gluttony in our society is not a simple temptation to overindulge in chocolate, or even to hoard our Easter eggs. When I consider the amount of emotional energy I have spent on dieting, I can hardly believe it. I remember spirals of guilt, making me feel so debilitated I could hardly pray. Sometimes when I'm worrying about my waistline, I tell myself, "Mary Ellen, do you realize how lucky you are? How many people through the last millennium were lucky enough to be concerned with overeating and pudginess?" Very few. Most dreaded catching the plague, getting deathly infections from small cuts, or dying in childbirth. And if they worried about food, it was usually getting enough food to survive, and that's still a problem for many people today.

The Horns of a Dilemma

The real problem with gluttony is not eating. Attacking (or even eliminating) overeating doesn't approach the real issue. Eating is often the least part of the problem compared to the guilt and condemnation women face from eating too much. Debilitated by guilt we feel useless and more unloved than before. And instead of asking why this behavior is happening, we condemn ourselves until we eat some more (for comfort) and then feel worse. If food were really only food, we wouldn't be facing such a predicament.

Women's magazines demonstrate our greater dilemma. On

their covers are luscious desserts, loaded with cream and chocolate. "Make this tempting dessert in only fifteen minutes!"
Beside the cover photo, headlines such as "Slimmer Hips in
Two Weeks," "Dr. Freddie's No-Pain Diet," and "Look the Way
You've Always Wanted to Look for Your High School Reunion"
seduce us. Food and body image do battle right there on the
cover!

Gluttony is a problem because food (for ourselves and our
families) and the perfect body are simultaneously flaunted. For
many women, eating competes with words and pictures describing the acceptable and ideal body.

Food and Body Image: My Story
Seven-year-old Susannah talks to me at the dining room table,
but really she's watching herself in the mirror on our side-
board. She cannot tear her eyes from the attractive creature
who flips her curly brown hair, twists and shakes her body.

From my earliest memories, I had trouble looking in mirrors.
I watched my mother in the bathroom mirror as she combed
her hair, lips pursed. She bobbed her hand, trying to get the
front hair to stand up just so. I never looked at myself; somehow
I couldn't show even my mother that I cared. I got pointy brown
glasses in second grade. They sat on my nose, making me stu-
dious, not pretty. And there were the pin curls that my mother
stuck around the sides of my head each night to try to make
my naturally straight hair curly. I didn't care; I got good grades
and read a lot.

I found an article in *McCall's* about child models. I kept it
folded in my diary. My favorite model had large blue eyes and
brown hair; her hair curved like that perfect loop a wave makes
before it crashes. I read and reread the commentary: "Debbie,
age eight, has been a model since she was two. She captures

that perfect, every hair in place look which so many magazines love. Her father is a surgeon in New York City and her mother acts as Debbie's agent." I named my doll Debbie and agreed to a Toni home permanent in June. During one of the "sets" I sat on a faded red chair in our side yard, eating toast with home-made raspberry jam on it, thinking about Debbie. After six hours of rollers and pungent solutions, my hair looked picture-perfect. I left my glasses off and squinted at the mirror. The next day my hair was flat and it was back to pin curls. "I think that permanent gave you just the extra bend you needed," my mother said.

In seventh grade the girls primped in front of the bathroom mirrors combing their bangs with water and Dippity-Doo so that they came below their tweezed eyebrows. "Oh, gross, a zit! Can I borrow some of your make-up?" I emerged from a stall, washed my hands and didn't glance at the mirror.

That same year Lisa and I spent some rainy spring vacation days looking at her father's *Playboy* magazines. "Look at this one: she's like a Barbie doll," I moaned to Lisa. Huge breasts, small waists, long legs. This is how our bodies were meant to look. Lisa wore a size B cup. I didn't need a bra at all, and my legs were kind of pudgy.

Twiggy appeared on the cover of *Life* magazine. "She's down-right ugly," said my mom. "No one wants a boyish woman," said my dad. One day in ninth grade, one of the skinniest girls, who wore clothes out of *Seventeen,* sighed and said, "I really have got to lose weight." "Where?" we asked. "Look," she said, tucking her leg back so she was sitting on her foot and indicating the slight bulge by her knee.

I started dieting. Two weeks of starvation and then two weeks of food binges—pizzas, burgers from Herfies, Cokes and ice cream. When I felt obese, I weighed myself—150, oh no—and put on my brother's track suit and ran four miles.

The summer before my senior year I biked six miles to my job at the library. I sat in the sun and slowly ate a small salad for lunch, noticing no difference in my hunger pangs after I had consumed it. I walked into the kitchen after work and found my mother taking blueberry muffins out of the oven. "Mom," I wailed, "how could you do this to me? Don't you know I'm trying to lose weight? I hate you!" I ran to my bedroom.

I felt the same emotion but was more practiced at politeness ten years later in South Africa, when one evening the door bell rang as I was settling down to read a book. There was a parishioner holding out a plate of cookies, beaming. "I brought you some cookies."

"Thank you so much. How kind of you," I said, thinking "How could you do this to me? Either I eat them all right now or spend the evening with my eyes floating over Jane Austen, my mind in the kitchen with the cookies."

After Stephen was born, I breastfed him and tried to eat a normal diet. I lost thirty pounds. I felt wonderful. All my clothes fell off me, and I had to buy new ones. I bought a jumpsuit that showed how slender my waist was, how thin my thighs were. My breasts were large from breastfeeding. I felt different about my body: at the age of twenty-eight I still wanted to look like a Barbie. Whom did I need to impress?

Even now when I'm having my hair cut and the hairdresser spins me around after the blow-dry and indicates I should admire myself in the mirror, I hesitate to ask for my glasses so that I can see the flesh and brown blur in the mirror. I do ask for my glasses but only so the hairdresser won't think I'm a fool: "What kind of woman doesn't have the guts to look at herself in the mirror when she's paying me twenty bucks for a haircut?"

What kind of woman indeed? One who still sees herself as

a little girl with pin curls and pointy glasses, who (like most women) has listened closely to the message that an acceptable body is all-important.

The Face in the Mirror

Do you like the image you see in the mirror? If you do, you are in a select minority. Of 33,000 women surveyed by *Glamour* only 6 percent felt satisfied with their bodies.[1] The majority of women overestimate their body size when describing themselves.[2] Because femaleness has not been valued by our culture, women are more subject to feelings of inferiority; therefore if they don't like what they see in the mirror, everything is affected.[3]

What the World Tells Women about Their Bodies

The correct body is dictated by societal standards, which Christians have called the world. The correct woman's body has always been the one that will help her be attractive to a man. Since styles change, this image also has changed. The ideal woman in Renaissance paintings differs from the image we are shown now. Rubens, Titian, Raphael and Michelangelo idealized women who would be laughed out of an aerobics class today.

In the first two decades of this century, a skinny body was seen as unattractive and unhealthy. With the twenties came the rise of the suffragette movement, and women wanted to look like men. It was "in" to be skinny, have short hair and even bind the breasts.

What is the late twentieth-century Western world's standard of beauty to which we all must attain? Fashion shows, advertisements and women's magazines communicate the ideal. Women require time and work to make themselves "presentable." What must a woman do to be beautiful? "She must diet to rid herself of ugly fat; curl, straighten, or dye her hair; learn to apply make-up; learn how to dress; learn how to sit, stand and walk in order to become acceptable. She must shave her legs and armpits, tweeze her eyebrows, bleach the hair on her arms and face in order to become acceptable. She must never forget perfume and deodorant."[4] A woman's body is not acceptable as it is; society does not accept it, and neither does she.

How can a woman accept her body when she is comparing it to an ideal that has little or no fat, is slightly athletic, long and lean, preferably large-busted? The ideal woman looks like a Barbie doll, and the message has been repeated to us through toys, cartoons, sitcoms and magazines from the time we were young. The perfect woman's body is judged (by a panel of men) in the swimsuit contest of the Miss America Contest (and its variations). But even this perfect woman must tape herself in certain places so she sticks out just right. The perfect woman's body hits us from mannequins in the stores, and especially in the media.

Even among the models and actresses, few women with perfect bodies exist. Computers touch up their photographs, technologically slimming thighs and heightening eyebrow bends. Or we see perfect detached parts: the perfect hand, the perfect thigh, the perfect ankle, the perfect eyebrow. Even if a normal woman had the right body type and was in no way predisposed genetically to be plump, she couldn't compete with the media's altered images of women.

The perfect body is adolescent and impossible to achieve, but we believe that we need that kind of body (or at least one that is close) to be truly acceptable. This intolerable pressure, to reject our bodies, to ignore our appetites as bad, is more unbearable for some women. At its worst it emerges in the self-loathing of anorexia or bulimia, conditions that are growing catastrophically among young people today. Some psychologists argue that anorexia is a teen's rejection of the womanhood she has seen consistently devalued.[5] It is not coincidence that most victims are women; they are the ones who are put under most pressure to conform to the standard of the perfect body.

Who are the losers? Women. We are the losers as we are tempted to invest our time and energy pursuing a mirage, chasing a standard set by the world. We are the losers when food looms out of proportion, and we are caught in a spiral of condemnation and despair. Most studies show that ninety percent of dieters who successfully lose weight gain it back. What an encouraging statistic *that* is! It points to a life of frustration for those obsessed by food and society's image of the perfect body. We are the losers when we allow our dislike of our bodies to drive us to do foolish things.

Who are the losers? Women are the losers as we waste our time, emotional energy and money. Once again (thanks to the flesh and the world, probably packaged by the devil) I try to replace Jesus at the center of my life with my beautiful body. When I lose weight and begin to look like *x*, then I will be happy; then I will be confident; then I will be a worthy person. We don't get on with living for Christ but worry about food and our shape instead. Satan must be delighted to have so much money, emotional energy and time spent pursuing the meaningless mirage of the ideal woman's body.

Who are the winners in this game? Mainly the fashion experts who can keep pushing different clothes and fancy make-ups to make us look better, to make us acceptable and happy. Another big winner is the diet industry. "Americans spent more than $30 billion last year on such offerings as diet books, videotapes, appetite suppressants, 'lite' foods, low-calorie beverages and commercial weight-loss programs."[6] Plastic surgeons and those who perform liposuction also make money on this obsession.

Free to Be Fat

The shelves of Christian books such as *Free to Be Thin, The Exodus Diet Plan, Thin, Trim, and Triumphant: How to Get God's Help in Losing Unwanted Pounds,* and *Flip Your Flab Forever* imply that societal standards of female beauty have seeped into the church. Paul suggests that Christians should not be conformed to the world (Rom 12:1-2). The pressure to conform is powerful; to not conform we must question the Barbie doll image and ask why a woman's body shape should be dictated by the world.

The worst disservice that "Christian diets" do for women is to imply that if women deal with an overeating problem and become the right shape (and thereby follow the instructions of the world, voiced through the diet plans and fashion moguls) they will be happy and fulfilled. That of course is idolatry; nothing but our relationship with God can make us fulfilled. According to Peter, a woman's beauty is something inward, not her outward shape (1 Pet 3:3).

Suggesting that Christian women can conform to the world's fashion statement by dieting applies a band-aid to a deep wound. Many "Christian" dieting books rub salt into that deep wound of a woman's low self-esteem by implying that fat can be equated with sin. Guilt added to a poor self-image is not helpful, and the accumulated weight of this guilt pulls a person into a deeper and deeper spiral of self-rejection. How many of us have snapped at our children or been irritable with a friend because we were feeling guilty and condemned about eating two brownies or because our dieting stomachs ached for food? And if the church regards fat, which is very visible, as an indication of sin, it should require all other sinners to wear some indication of their sins, like *The Scarlet Letter*'s *A* for adultery. People should wear big *P*'s for pride or huge *L*'s for lust.

Breaking the Cycle

To see how thoroughly the world has seeped into the church, we need only look at some Christian books about marriage, which underline the world's idea of beauty.

In *His Needs, Her Needs* Willard Harley discusses one of man's greatest needs in a chapter entitled: "He Needs a Good-Looking Wife—An Attractive Spouse." Harley talks about Nancy, a woman who gained weight after her marriage to Harold. Harold, of course, cannot handle the fact that his wife is not attractive, that he is not proud to be seen with her. In counseling this man, Harley suggests a legal separation. "Tell her the separation will remain in effect until she loses her weight."[7] Fortunately, Nancy gets motivated and goes on a diet. She loses weight and Harold can come back. Once again he can be proud to be with her as she fulfills his male need for an attractive spouse. She must feel very secure and happy to have a man who cares about her so deeply and unconditionally!

The world's influence must have caused Harley to forget that in marriage we promise to live with each other, for better and for worse.

Later in the same chapter, Harley suggests that a woman pay attention to her make-up, pointing out what a disaster it can be if a woman has made herself up nicely and forgotten to tweeze her eyebrows. (How shocking!) He recommends cosmetic surgery for prematurely wrinkled women, although it does have to be repeated every few years. It's disturbing to see "Christian counselors" suggesting that a man's "needs" take precedence over biblical messages about beauty. How thoroughly the world has seeped into the church.

We must reject the world's standard of beauty, even if we encounter it in the church. No person worth worrying about would love you more with a perfect body. Am I really convinced that I would be more truly loved and lovable if I looked like a model? The sin in gluttony may be more in not trusting God's love for us, in selling out to society's standards of what makes people good and important.

And this affects the fat or the thin. Thin people can become subject to pride; they can feel proud of their bodies, superior to those who struggle with weight. Or people who feel they are too skinny can go through the same self-loathing as those who feel too fat. God certainly wouldn't love us more if our bodies were perfect. One woman wrote that after she thought about having a perfect body and then looked at herself in the mirror, she thought, "I have a woman's body. There is nothing wrong with softness and curves."

The great Christian writer Dorothy L. Sayers wrote this in answer to men who didn't like women wearing trousers because it was unattractive: "If the trousers do not attract you, so much the worse: for the moment I do not want to attract you. I want to enjoy myself as a human being."[8] The world will tell us that how we look to men is of the utmost importance. If we have bought into the world's image of female beauty, we must divest ourselves of it. There is no satisfaction to be had in a beautiful body; our only contentment is to be found in God.

If we can begin to peel off the layers of society's preaching, "Thou shalt be skinny or condemned," then food can become food. When we are dealing simply with whether or not to eat a piece of chocolate cake and not with mountains of guilt, condemnation and a perfect image gloating at us, our view of ourselves becomes much more manageable. If we keep pushing ourselves to make physical changes, we should ask, "Why? What am I trying to prove, and to whom?"

Other Kinds of Gluttony

There are other variations on gluttony, other temptations to allow food to assume huge proportions in our lives. These also shift us away from the biblical perspective where we thank God for providing food for us and also give some away.

Sometimes as the main food preparer in our families, we can "need to be needed" so that we over-emphasize the food that we put on the table. We may spend hours in preparation and baking, making more food than the family can (or should) eat. If it matters to me a whole lot whether people think I'm an amazingly good cook or baker extraordinaire, I need to ask myself why I am investing so much in this area of my life.

C. S. Lewis writes about another kind of gluttony in *The Screwtape Letters*, where the glutton "gives a little scream at the plate which some overworked waitress has set before her and says, 'Oh, that's far, far too much! Take it away and bring me about a quarter of it.' " Lewis points out that she is a victim to the "all-I-want" mentality, which is an insatiable demand for the perfect boiled egg, or the perfect piece of toast, which she thinks she remembers from the past.[9]

Or there is the kind of gluttony that is associated with gourmet eating, seeking more and more exotic food to eat, more expensive mushrooms, more extraordinary restaurants. This kind of super-sophistication tempts us to overemphasize food and can lead to a sense of superiority. Can a Christian in good conscience spend $15.99 a pound for Shitakane mushrooms when people are starving in the world?

Another very contemporary kind of gluttony is what I call "salvation by food." We are stewards of our bodies and should eat good, healthy food, but it is possible to exaggerate this so that we begin to believe that if we eat healthy food, and provide for our family the right food, we will live (practically) forever. We congratulate ourselves for our own good health or the health of our family; we have taken responsibility for our own salvation.

Ten years ago a young Christian woman named Diane had cancer. Many people prayed for Diane as she had surgery. Through the influence of another Christian couple, Bill and Daphne, Diane went on a special diet that allowed no refined sugar. I talked to Bill and Daphne, two years after Diane's diagnosis, as we ate whole wheat toast and strawberry jam, sweetened with honey. "How's Diane?" I asked.

"Much better," responded Daphne. "Thanks to a sugar-free diet."

I was stunned. I could understand it if this woman had told me that they weren't sure whether it was diet or prayer or what. I could also understand that in the stress of seeing a person suffering from a disease that seems so unreasonable, the desire to have some control, to do something, must be very strong. But for them to assume that they had somehow brought about Diane's healing through substituting honey for sugar in her diet seemed to me to be idolatry. Although we are to be responsible stewards, we cannot take our salvation into our own hands. That is taking God's place, saving our health and our lives through food.

Don't get me wrong. There may be times when, to be good stewards of our bodies, we should lose weight. While we cannot totally guard our own health, we are to treat our bodies as temples of the Holy Spirit and not misuse them. And self-control is a fruit of the Spirit. There may be practical reasons to watch our weight. I'm watching my waistline at the moment because I don't want to expand out of my clothes and have to buy new ones. But I'm not doing it because I think I need to look attractive, because my husband or children will love me more, or because God will love me more.

Our appearance can have such a hold on us that we forget what is really important. Women often continue to smoke so that they won't gain weight. Tanning seems important, even though it is dangerous. Studies have found that forty percent of those who undergo surgery for skin cancer resume identical tanning habits afterwards. Women wear high heels that hurt their feet and backs. Women try so hard to find fulfillment through their appearance that they lose sight of what really makes them worthy.

Freedom: Erica's Story

Erica is an unusual person. She is confident, jovial and a highly qualified doctor. She is friendly and laughs a lot. She has the air of a person who really knows who she is and is happy about it. She has been a Christian for a number of years.

Erica is slightly overweight, but perhaps her outstanding feature is her face. She has probably thirty raised moles on her face.

She worked at a mission hospital in Uganda for a number of years. During that time, a man, maybe fifty years old, was brought in from the outlying districts very seriously ill with malaria. Erica worked with him over several weeks and they got to be friends, although she couldn't speak his particular dialect. When the great day came and he was well enough to go home, his family traveled to get him. His brother spoke Swahili as well as his native dialect so he could interpret.

"He says how very much he wishes to thank you," the brother translated the old man's words. "And he says he is very sorry about your face."

"My face?" Erica asked in Swahili.

The old man spoke again and the brother translated. "Your moles. He says he's sorry about the ugliness of your moles."

"Tell him not to mind," Erica said. "In my country they are a sign of great beauty."

In Erica's true country, which is heaven, her face is indeed one of great beauty as she is so given to her Lord and knows securely how she is loved by God. That is true freedom.

6/FILLING OUR LIVES WITH THE TRIVIAL

W *hen I was twenty-two my new husband and I moved to Cape* Town, South Africa. Ernie was a confident twenty-nine-year-old with a doctorate in genetics, besides his seminary training. Ten days after we arrived, he was ordained as a minister to work in the Anglican church in Cape Town. He began the visiting, preaching and meetings that were his job.

I experienced culture shock. We had been living in a one-bedroom apartment in Bellingham, Washington; now I had a five-bedroom rectory to furnish. I had to learn to drive our VW "beetle" on the wrong side of the road and figure out what supermarket products were equivalent to American products. I discovered that what is cornstarch in the United States and cornflour in England is Maizena in South Africa.

I felt overwhelmed, so I used my time to do what I knew I could do well. I made my own granola, peanut butter and bread. When Andrew was born I made baby food in the blender, decorated his room and made dungarees for him with patchwork motifs on the front. On a modest curate's salary I sewed cushions, quilted wall-hangings, curtains and lampshades. At Christmas time, I scrambled to get hold of American Christmas issues of *McCall's, Better Homes and Gardens* and *Good Housekeeping.* I wanted to make magic Christmas memories for the children: tiny felt ice skates, appliqued doll ornaments, counted cross-stitch wreaths, nutshell cradles. I made a gingerbread house, patchwork wreaths and Christmas presents such as pincushions, tissue holders, small bags, not only for family and friends but also for the crowd who came to us for Christmas dinner. I was busy, very busy. But I never stopped to ask myself whether I was using my time and talents responsibly.

What's important in our lives gets squeezed out by that which keeps us frantically busy. People call this the "tyranny of the urgent." I've heard preachers and time management experts hold forth on this "tyranny"; they advise that the urgent be examined and eliminated so that what's truly important can be fulfilled. What do they expect women to do? Leave the children at their French horn lessons? Cook in a house without groceries? Let their family wear mismatched socks? The preacher and time management expert were probably not thinking about women. Women's lives have so consistently been filled with frantic activities that most of us know no other way to live.

What do we think of when we think of sloth? Laziness, usually. The Bible talks a bit about laziness, mostly in Proverbs and Ecclesiastes, where the lazy are told to get off their backsides and take a cue from the ant. "Go the ant, you lazybones; consider its ways, and be wise" (Prov 6:6). Some people are lazy; they love to sit around, feet up, watching TV. But most of us have been so deeply affected by the Protestant work ethic that we suffer more from frantic activity than too little activity. Sitting around for hours is not even a temptation for most women I know; there's not time even to consider it.

Originally *sloth* meant "spiritual lethargy." Sloth implied that a person was lazy about Christian growth. The New Testament zeroes in on spiritual laziness. Jesus told his followers, "Do not work for the food that perishes, but for the food that endures for eternal life, which the Son of Man will give you" (Jn 6:27). Christians are counseled to "not become sluggish" but "imitators of those who through faith and patience inherit the promises" (Heb 6:12). When I don't bother to spend time with God or don't care about my relationship with God, when I allow other activities to take priority over my relationship with God, then I am tempted by sloth. I am replacing God with my frantic activity.

Tempted by sloth, we are tempted to forget that our time and talents are gifts from God to be used for him. We begin to believe that time is ours to kill or fill at our own discretion. We forget Paul's words: "You are not your own . . . you were bought with a price" (1 Cor 6:20). The master said to the slave who has buried his talent: "You wicked and lazy slave!" (Mt 25:26). Why was the master angry? The slave had not used his talent as a responsible steward. The temptation of sloth for many of us is to fill our time with the urgent—to not use our time and talents responsibly.

Squeezing God Out
Three years ago I went for my day of silent prayer at a retreat

center near our church. I spent three or four hours in silent prayer and Bible reading, and some time just sitting in God's presence. Suddenly it hit me: "I have been a Christian nearly twenty years. I have been to thousands of hours of Bible study, and that has been great. I have spent hours telling God what he ought to do for me and others. What's worse, I have spent days cleaning house and weeks baking. I wonder how many trivial little bags I have sewn or how many hours of mindless novels I have endured? And I have *never before* spent this much time quiet with God, listening for what he would say to me." Needless to say, God did have plenty to say to me, after trying to get through for nearly twenty years and always finding the line busy!

"The greatest sin is prayerlessness," writes P. T. Forsyth.[1] Prayerlessness is the sin of which I have been most guilty. I have always wanted to pray, always thought I should pray, but I have consistently filled my life with things other than prayer, have constantly allowed my busyness to push out time with God.

The world gives messages about what is important. Our accomplishments, our money, our shape, we are told, are vastly important. These are general messages, but women have often been told that their time is not as valuable as men's time. And women have come to believe society's message.

Devalued
The media portrays women's time as less important. A woman's great feats are often related to cleaner, sparkling windows. Society as a whole rewards its women in the workplace much less than its men. Men's time must be more valuable—why else would women make an average of sixty-seven cents for every dollar paid to men for the same job?

I know a few men who are house-husbands. They tell me that

people often say, "When are you going to do some real work?" or "Don't you miss having a real job?" People used to say to women, "Oh you're only a housewife, only a homemaker?" They seldom say that anymore, but if one person is going to spend time at home with the children it should be the woman because her time is less inherently valuable than her husband's.

The traditional work of a woman (the job of the homemaker) is reckoned by our culture as relatively unimportant. Child-rearing, from the world's point of view, is not really crucial; it doesn't bring in any loot, so how could it be strategic? (Congress has trouble passing any parental leave plans, implying that parents caring for children in their first months of life would be a terrible waste of time and money.)

The church is often affected by the message of the world. Within the church itself, women have often been encouraged to fill their lives with the trivial.

A friend of mine took her mother to the spring tea at their church. The speaker brought her collection of one hundred stuffed bunnies, which she uses for her talks at various Christian women's organizations. The speaker displays her bunny collection at the front, and then tells stories using the bunnies. There is a white bunny who represents the good, Christian rabbit and there is a black bunny who needs to repent and find Jesus. Her talk lasts twenty minutes or so, and afterwards the women can go up and look at the bunnies. My friend said she heard a chorus of women's voices: "Oh, aren't they so cute!"

Don't get me wrong; I love bunnies, too. But the church can easily underline the world's message about the value of women's time by sponsoring trivial meetings. Then the church becomes guilty of leading women into temptation, the temptation to fill our time with the trivial. We may hardly even notice such activities and the message that they are giving women.

Try to imagine yourself as a Christian woman from another country, like Zaire for instance. You have been actively involved in ministry there and are now visiting this country.

You walk into a church service on Sunday morning. At the front of the church there are only men who lead the worship, read the Scriptures, pray and preach. You might think that this is a church for men only, but you see many women in the pews, more than men, in fact.

Then you look in the bulletin; here are opportunities for women! You see that you could go to a women's group and learn to make Christmas decorations and next week you could learn your "color season"! That's not all; you scan the page further down and see some ministries you know are important: you could look after children in the nursery and teach Sunday School (at least up until children reach a certain magic age). You could also help serve a meal for some homeless people and pray for missionaries.

Some trivial and some important activities would be available to you as a woman. How would it be different if you were a man? If you were a man, you could attend a prayer breakfast and hear a speaker talk on "Paul's theology of judgment." You could stand up at the front and read a lesson or lead prayers. There are few opportunities for service, few for working with children. There is no opportunity for a man to learn about his color season or about making Christmas tree decorations. As a woman, attending this church even once, you have been told that your time is assumed to be less valuable than a man's.

The world and the world in the church have given us a clear message: a woman's time is less valuable. Satan is obviously delighted if he can encourage over half of all church members to fritter their time in trivial, frantic activity.

Servanthood Squeeze

Sally was a rector's wife in England. Her husband's study was in their home, so she often made a cup of tea and offered cookies to the person who was waiting to see the vicar next. She found it difficult to concentrate on her reading or writing because she was constantly interrupted. Still she had read about being a servant for Christ, and she practiced her servanthood well.

One day her husband rushed in, asked for some supper, then raced to his study to finish a talk he had to give that night. Sally suddenly wondered, "What would it be like if Nigel spent every waking hour making cups of tea for people? Then he'd be the Christlike servant? No he wouldn't. He'd be seen as wasting his time and his gifts. Maybe I'm wasting my gifts." Sally realized that she considered her time less valuable than her husband's. She realized that in believing this she was buying in to the world's judgment of what is important.

Sally confronted her husband. Nigel could see that he had been taking advantage of her willingness to serve, and that as a result she had never found a ministry of her own. Sally now has a wonderful counseling ministry, where her caring and listening skills are really used.

Servanthood involves finding our gifts and offering them for the good of the body of Christ.

Sometimes women have allowed the call to servanthood to let them off the hook of using their God-given gifts. We have associated servanthood with doing the mundane. Sally, with her innumerable cups of tea for parishioners, realized that in acting as she thought a servant should, she was actually being irresponsible toward herself and her husband.

Roberta Hestenes, president of Eastern Baptist College, has also experienced the dilemma of servanthood:

As a woman, I have struggled with that whole image because it is hard to be a servant when everyone expects you to be. I was in a meeting with about fifty men and I think there were two women in the room. I was in charge of one section of the meeting but only two other people in the room knew that. The opening statement was, "Now let's see, we need someone who can take notes." Fascinating the way every eye in the room turns to the women. . . . Sometimes we have to say no in certain settings. But always, we are called to servant-hood, not because the people we serve deserve it, but because Jesus Christ deserves it.[2]

Often women serve, not because "Christ deserves it," but because they need to be needed. It is essential to their sense of well-being.

"Mom, get me some water," a nine-year-old shouts at the potluck. "Mom, I want some water."

"Don't you think you could get the water yourself?" I ask.

"Oh yeah, but she'll get it for me," he replies. Sure enough, she walks in and hands him the water. He smiles at me and winks.

There was a time when this child needed Mom to get him water; often women continue to nurture when it is no longer helpful. We need to be needed. This kind of giving has a dark shadow, the shadow of a woman's need to feel worthy. We can find ourselves giving out of our own emotional thirst. When a woman finds herself tidying up after children who could clean their own rooms, driving them back to school to get the homework they forgot or getting the glass of water for the nine-year-old, she needs to ask herself why.

Perhaps we have bought the world's view of our time. Perhaps we are unsure of ourselves and our self-images are low, so we find it very difficult to say no. If we're having a cup of tea in a restaurant and the waiter asks us if we want something else, we sometimes feel we really ought to order. Or we hate to disappoint a friend at a Tupperware party. Or if someone phones and asks us to teach Sunday School, we don't stop and weigh our gifts and our time. We feel we ought to say yes. Of course, then our time will fill to overflowing with things to do.

When I reflect on my years in Cape Town, I have mixed feelings. It was wonderful to be able to totally immerse myself in the children, to be totally at their disposal. But when I look at all the hours I spent baking and sewing, I see it as a tremendous waste. Not that I think baking and sewing are inherently wasteful; I still spend time in those activities. But I realize that the only reason someone would bake and sew as whole-heartedly as I did would be to prove something. I really wanted to prove something.

For me (and I believe for many women) saying yes to everyone, cooking and baking and sewing, making innumerable cups of tea, became a way of winning approval. If I breastfed perfectly, baked the perfect loaf of bread, put on the ideal five-course meal, sewed clothes for my family, made presents for anyone who crossed my path and decorated my house so that it looked like a picture from *Better Homes and Gardens* then I must be a good person.

Of course, it didn't work. The trivial doesn't satisfy, and I felt worse and worse about what I had to offer. I lost a sense of having any gifts, having any ability to change anything (I can't really do anything about apartheid or the homeless squatters or the feeding scheme in the squatter area, I'm too busy making pincushions). I thought I was being wonderfully selfless—"Here's a little something I made you; you see it's a mending pincushion, and the pattern is taken from an antique one at Matjiesfontein. It's a scrap of Liberty Lawn I had left over; I'm so glad you like it." That was all done to build me up, to make me feel good, to encourage people to say, "That Mary Ellen is such a gifted seamstress, and what a mother."

Our lives often revolve around the home and family and meals and carpools and clothes. Homemaking can be a wonderful skill as we use our nurturing gifts to make the home a pleasant place. But we need to think carefully before we give homemaking the kind of blessing that it has often received in middle-class America. I knew a woman who felt she couldn't leave her house until it was spotless. She couldn't meet me until the burners on her stove were clean; she felt bad leaving a mess. Decorating can soak up hours and money, as we pore over magazines, visit home decorating stores, sew cushions and put up wallpaper. Nowhere in the New Testament do we see this kind of emphasis on the home promoted.

I made choices about how I would use my time in South Africa. I missed opportunities for deep relationships, for involvement with the poor and oppressed, for development of my gifts, for time with God. I had no time for silence, for deepening roots of spirituality, for reaching toward God. I couldn't invest myself in the unseen, such was my need for approval.

What Is Really Important
A woman who is a well-known teacher and leader told me about a turning point in her life:

I had a baby who was under a month old, and I was tired. I went to a women's retreat and I had to take the baby with me. I was spiritually hungry—my father had died and it had been difficult. I desperately needed to hear this speaker, and the baby cried. I had to leave the room. And I was weeping because I was spiritually needy. The pastor's wife left the group and came and took the baby—it makes me weep to remember—and said, "You go back in and listen." And her service changed my life. It was such a small gesture . . . and she does not know but her willingness to take that baby out of my arms and to comfort my baby (who's now my handsome grown son) so that I could listen to the speaker teach the Scriptures, was a gift that changed my life.

This woman realized that both the speaker (who was a godly, competent and attractive woman) and the pastor's wife (doing a very womanly thing) equally helped meet her spiritual need and set her direction toward Christian leadership.[3]

When we believe the world, we regard some people's time as more important than others. Politicians have a way of greeting you with one eye on your face and the other over your shoulder, seeing if someone more important (richer, more powerful, more intelligent) is standing beyond you.

Jesus gave each person his total attention, recognizing each as valuable. He was known for spending time with outcasts: tax-collectors, women of ill repute, the poor. Jesus was not snowed by the exteriors of those he met, holy or otherwise. Especially in our culture we look at the outside. People are important because we've seen them on TV, because they are rich and live in a fabulous neighborhood, because they are beautiful and model for a magazine, or because they are high up in a corporation or politics. God sees our time as equally important, whether we are vice-president of a multinational corporation, a famous movie star, a homemaker, or a janitor. Our time is a gift from God to be used as carefully as possible for him. This will include prayer, putting on the mind of Christ through study and doing other things to which he calls us.

The world wants to see success. God's priorities may not be so glittery. In our efforts to live strategic lives for God, we cannot take our cue from the world, which would assure us that only the rich and beautiful and powerful and well-educated are important. Think of God's strategy of allowing Jesus to be born in a stable, to live with the poor, touching the lives of the weak.

Henri Nouwen, a Roman Catholic scholar and writer, talks about his experiences at Jean Vanier's L'Arche communities, where so-called normal people give themselves to care for the mentally handicapped. Nouwen suggests that we need to be open to "wasting time with God and the poor people of God."[4]

The Martha Mentality

I imagine myself at Bethany one morning. I am Martha. My sister Mary and I have just heard that Jesus will be arriving soon.

"Mary, quick, get the shrimp out of the freezer, and I think I'll do a paella; everybody loved it the other day when I made it. But I've got to get some green peppers; maybe I've got some in the fridge, and where is my saffron? Oh, no, there's the door now. Mary, will you grab that?

"Hi Jesus, come on in . . . make yourself at home, I'm just throwing together a little lunch. Want some punch? It'll just take a minute.

"Okay, the lemons for the punch, whirl that in the blender with the ice . . . this should be refreshing . . . I wish I had a starter; I've got that Brie and some chutney . . . perfect. I'll run the punch in and then take in the hors d'oeuvres . . . but first let me get the rice going for the paella, and what about dessert? Oh no, I'm out of ice cream and I think Lazarus finished off the last of that cake. But that lime dessert is quick to make and on such a hot day it'd be perfect . . . where's the recipe . . . but let me run this punch in.

"Punch for you both . . . I'll bring the starter in a minute . . . you're welcome.

"Okay the chutney on the Brie and the crackers at the edge
. . . Mary just sitting there, next to Jesus, listening to him as if
she has all the time in the world . . . and me in here slaving
. . . that's why she has all the time in the world. I hope Jesus
realizes that I'm being the servant. Mom would like it . . . she'd
say to me, 'Good work, Martha, got to feed them well to keep
them happy,' that's what she'd say. But you'd think Mary would
at least make the dessert. Where's the butter and I've got to juice
three limes . . . why do I do all the work around here when she
just sits there? And I'm getting hot, too. And it'll be an hour at
this rate till we can eat. I'll just take this in to them.

"Here's something for you to nibble on. You're welcome. But,
Lord, don't you care that my sister has left me to do the work
by myself? Tell her to help me!"

"Martha, Martha, you are worried and distracted by many
things; there is need of only one thing. Mary has chosen the better part, which will not be taken away from her" (Lk 10:38-42).

How did Martha feel when Jesus said this to her? How would
we feel if Jesus challenged us to stop our frantic activity and
listen to him? I think it must have taken Martha months to
accept that all her frantic "good" activities, the servantlike emphasis on food and home, were not truly important.

Martha may have asked herself (as we should ask ourselves)
why she was investing herself in such frantic activity. Many
women feel they have no choice, that they are victims in their
life. Many single parents who must work do have fewer choices.
But we need to stop being victims to the urgent and look at the
way we are spending our lives.

Perhaps Martha looked closely at her life and realized just
how much time she was spending on fancy meals and home
decorating. If we keep track of how we are actually spending
our time, we sometimes find some surprises. We may find that

driving kids to hockey takes ten hours a week; maybe that needs to be cut. We may find that we watch more television than we had ever guessed. Statistics show that most people far underestimate the time spent in front of the television and far overestimate the time they spend with their children.

Martha wouldn't have been able to test herself on what I believe may be the best "frantic busyness" test:

On December 20th, how do you usually feel?

☐ Frantic: desperately trying to finish making and buying presents, wrapping gifts, making taffy and gingerbread houses.

☐ Busy: school concerts, services and a few packages to get.

☐ Totally laid back: everything is just about ready.

Although few of us achieve the "totally laid back" attitude, our Christmas activity level may indicate how we have been taken in by sloth, how much we fill our lives with the trivial. We can hardly appreciate the significance of God's break into history because we've traded our peace and perspective for the world's view of how people have to *make* Christmas happen.

I wonder if Martha, after Jesus spoke to her, thought about her talents, too. The Bible clearly teaches that the way we have invested our time and talents will be judged (1 Cor 3:10-15). I imagine standing before God on the Judgment Day, shuffling my feet:

"Well, Sir, you're absolutely right that I didn't use my teaching gifts, but I made some terrific potholders . . . you're not really interested in those? My house was immaculate . . . looked like something out of *Better Homes and Gardens* . . . I think I have some pictures here . . . oh, that's not what you had in mind? But I sure got the impression from our church leaders that this was the sort of thing I ought to be doing . . . oh, you'll take care of *them* separately? I see."

We can be sure that Martha tried to spend time with Jesus,

that she listened to Jesus as she had seen her sister do. We can be sure that as we establish God's priorities in our lives, one top priority will be time to grow in our relationship with God.

I have found establishing a day's silent retreat each month to be absolutely essential. (Joyce Huggett's *The Joy of Listening to God* is very helpful for starting this habit.[5]) Besides the silence and prayer and Bible reading, I take time to check and see how my priorities are working out in my life. If I say my family is important to me but haven't been giving them much time, that has got to change. When we invest time with God, we begin to feel more whole in him. We feel clearer on how he wants us to spend our time and talents. This makes it easier for us to establish priorities and say no when we ought to.

We must look to God. The world had given Martha poor advice: "Turn out great meals for guests; no time to listen to Jesus." The world will give us poor advice: "Do one hundred percent womanly things all the time" or "Never do womanly things; those are useless." We must listen to God.

In a time of silence, slowly read the story about Martha and Mary (Lk 10:38-42) and contemplate what Jesus would say to you. After you think about the story, put your name in the words of Jesus: "_____ , you are worried and distracted by many things; there is need of only one thing." Tell God that you want to make time for that which is truly important.

7/LETTING OUR ANGER CONSUME US

Ann and her husband are active in an organization that helps elderly shut-ins in rural Wisconsin. The organization flew a speaker in for a weekend. After all the flurry of baking and meetings, Ann planned to take the speaker to the airport in Madison and at the same time visit a friend. Just before she was to leave, Ann's husband told her that he had been talking with the speaker and they had decided she was too tired to make the trip. She should stay home and rest, and they would arrange for someone else to drive him to Madison.

Ann was furious. But she was unable to direct her anger. She couldn't be angry at the speaker, who was in a position of authority. It would have been scary to be angry at her husband because anger didn't fit into Ann's categories of emotions that a "good" Christian should experience, or that a "good" wife should feel toward her husband.

So Ann cried her rage—at the people in that town who should have attended the meetings but hadn't. Not many people had come to the weekend. After all their work. How could they let her down like that?

We will get angry. People will treat us in ways that make us angry; our children or parents or friends will be treated in ways that make us angry; politicians and world affairs will make us angry. The Bible sees anger as a fact of life. Paul wrote to the Christians at Ephesus, "Be angry but do not sin" (Eph 4:26).

Anger is not a temptation, but anger can move us into three damaging temptations. The first is the temptation not to recognize our anger and deal with it. The second is the temptation to say or do things in our anger that we will later wish we hadn't. The third is to nurse our anger into bitterness and hatred.

Righteous Indignation
People often comment to me (sometimes even people I think I know quite well) about my gentleness. Once a woman said, as we dried teacups in a church kitchen, "Mrs. Ashcroft, you have a very godly bearing." Comments like these bother me, not because I'm very humble but because I don't feel gentle at all. My emotions roar inside me, especially my anger. For many years I had no idea what to make of my anger.

Sometimes my anger was righteous indignation, and living in South Africa can stir up lots of that. Once the South African government sent bulldozers into townships to flatten people's shacks, and I saw the streams of desperate faces, blank eyes, disoriented, almost dizzy expressions. I was furious and made a bumper sticker for my car that read "The Afrikaner Government are the illegal aliens. Bus *them* off somewhere!" I taped it to our '72 VW.

Two days later I was dropping children off at school. "Although I agree with your sentiments," a woman said, "someone will put a bomb under your car. I wanted to warn you." I took the sign off. I was angry, but I realized that venting my anger was probably not worth endangering the lives of my children.

Not-So-Righteous Indignation

My psychologist friend tells me that most of the women she sees are angry, although it often takes months of therapy for them to realize it. They may be angry because they feel devalued by their husbands and families, but they know that a good wife should not feel angry. They may be furious at God: God has let them down by not answering their deep-seated desires for a man to complete their lives. But no, they can't be mad at God—good women don't get angry, especially at God. Often we stuff our anger down inside, and it surfaces later as depression or bitterness. I have experienced this kind of anger in my life.

One Sunday evening I had gotten Andrew in bed and sat down to breastfeed Stephen. I had just opened my book when the phone rang.

Suddenly, I felt violated. Why should I have to put up with scores of phone calls a day because I was a minister's wife? Why should I politely answer the door to tramps who smelled of booze and demanded money for train tickets? Or why did I have to give cups of tea to weeping women whose husbands had left them and make sure the house was always tidy for parishioners? I got to the phone, picked it up and threw it down the stairs. It buzzed helplessly for a minute and then went dead.

I had a laugh later that evening with a few friends about the phone. The story about the phone circulated through the parish and amazed people. I was never sure whether they had trouble putting that incident together with the minister's wife they knew or whether it was just too amazing that a woman should throw a phone down the stairs. What seems odd to me now is the fact that I never really stopped to ask why I threw the phone down the stairs. I did it, and it felt great and that was that. The real reason for that anger, which was the tip of an iceberg, only came out seven or eight years later.

Women and Anger

Women have been taught from childhood not to fight or get angry. Studies of children's play show boys competing (both physically and verbally) and fighting. Girls tend to play cooperatively; they work hard to resolve differences. Compromise is the key to girls' play. "Okay, you can be the princess this time, and I'll be the prince; but next time we switch around, okay?"

Women also grow up maintaining relationships at almost any cost; a woman compromises, protects the male ego, pours oil on troubled waters, soothes emotions so that everyone gets along well. Most of us have the memory of a mother or grandmother saying, "Now dears, let's try to get along . . . let's don't talk about that now, it might upset him." We try desperately not to rock the boat. Our society has names for women who do rock the boat, for women who get angry—and those names are not used in polite company. How often do we find ourselves apologizing for something that is not our fault, just to keep people happy?

We often carry in our minds two images of women: the gentle mother and the nagging shrew. The gentle mother "pours oil on troubled water" and is always willing to give in for the sake of others. She never sits down at the table until halfway through a meal because she is making sure everyone is happy. She constantly quiets others' tempers so that no one gets hurt. We can't imagine her expressing any anger. The nagging shrew is always disagreeable and dissatisfied. Her anger ruins the peace and happiness of the home. Because we carry these two images in our heads, we have no model of an angry, good woman. We feel our choices are "no anger" or "destructive anger."[1] Because relationships are so important to women and anger appears to be such an overwhelming and potentially destructive emotion, we are afraid of it.

If this is true for women in general, how much more is it true for Christian women? Anger seems to be miles from the submissive, servantlike ideal required of Christian women. A famous series of lectures for Christians defines anger this way: "Not yielding up my rights to God." This definition does nothing to help resolve anger but complicates the matter with guilt.

Denying our anger may *seem* to lead us away from temptation. But actually, by not recognizing our anger we set ourselves up to sin. Our denied anger doesn't disappear. My psychologist friend tells of helpless women who come to her saying things like "He really hurt my feelings" or "I get so upset and depressed when he. . . ." These women are not recognizing their anger, so it is surfacing in more passive (and thus more acceptable) depression. When we repress angry feelings we complicate the issues and add to our problems. Instead we need to look carefully at our anger, recognize what it is telling us and find healthy ways of dealing with it so that it doesn't turn into sin.

Part of recognizing our anger is discovering what we are truly angry about, writes Harriet Lerner in her helpful book *The Dance of Anger.*[2] I was not really angry about the phone ringing that evening in the rectory when I threw it down the stairs. I wasn't even really angry at the demands that were being made of me; I had to look deeper to find the source of my anger.

Three years ago I learned what my anger was really about. I was teaching and studying while the children were in school for much of each day. South Africa seemed light-years away, although we'd only moved from Cape Town five years before. I started working on a short story about a Christmas dinner in Cape Town. I described the traditional English Christmas dinner that I cooked (in the heat of a Cape Town summer) and the guests (mainly British expatriate whites) who were invited. When our one black guest arrived with an unexpected entourage of his friends, I faced a dilemma: did I upset the party and make the Christmas dinner multiracial, or did I bow to the wishes of the people at the party who didn't want their dinner disrupted?

As I wrote the story, I realized I had known I wanted a disruptive, multiracial Christmas dinner, but instead of deciding that, I had asked my husband to make the decision. He was exhausted from four Christmas morning services and tactfully explained to the black guest that we couldn't fit them all around the table. I deferred to my husband's judgment that so many extras would throw the whole meal into chaos.

I worked for several weeks on the short story, basing it on this incident, and then I turned it in. My teacher's comment on the short story surprised me: "There's a lot of anger in this. Do you realize that the husband character in this is the villain?"

I reread the story. As I did my anger burned off the page. I realized that the story was not about the iniquity of apartheid but about being a woman in a society where I was treated as a child and consented to being treated as a child. It was anger at Ernie who had been quite *willing* to make the decision and *allowed* me to defer to it. It was about the kind of person I had been who had consented to being treated as a child, and in fact invited it, because that was what was going on in the society around me.

My anger blazed. That evening I handed the story to my husband. He read it slowly. He looked up at the end. "Hey. I'm the villain in this."

"You are," I said. "Because you were the villain. Or one of the villains. I'm just realizing how angry I was. I mean, I am." For several days I raged about the lack of selfhood that I had experienced there. Ernie agreed with me. I knew now why I had thrown the phone down the stairs.

Lashing Out

Although we must learn to recognize our anger, we need to be responsible for not allowing it to become destructive. Expressing our anger in the heat of the moment at a child, a spouse, or a friend can do irreparable damage. Often we need to wait an hour or two before expressing anger at the person we are angry at.

I know a family that has a time-out whistle. When one family member gets upset at another, he or she (either literally or figuratively) blows the whistle on the other. The one explains his or her anger or grievance. The other has to listen without interrupting, listen until he or she can explain verbally why the other is angry. This brings resolution and removes the possibility of bitterness from the anger. Each family member can "be angry" without sinning.

Maria made me angry one day after church. My blood boiled. I went home and thought about why I was so angry and how I could best tell her about it. I knew that if I didn't express my anger to her it would hurt our friendship.

I phoned her the next day, "I felt really mad at you yester-day."

"What did I do?" she asked.

"You sounded so superior when you talked about why you weren't going to that meeting about the church's involvement in the ghetto. As if you were above it. I felt like it was so easy for you to say . . . you're not a minister's wife who has to try to help inform people that are at different levels of awareness. You spoke as if you didn't know how I felt about it at all."

There was a silence. And then my friend spoke. "I can see how you might have felt that way. I'm sorry. Though I didn't really mean it like that. Forgive me."

Our relationship was healed and could go on.

Often we think, "I could never tell them about my anger." Sometimes it would be inappropriate to express our anger to a child or parent. There are many times when I feel like making my teenager sit while I say, "I am angry at you because you only think of yourself and your wants. You are acting like a thirteen-year-old, and it makes me very cross." All true but not very helpful. He can't see it at this stage. There are times when I express my anger to him and times when I need to keep my mouth shut.

When I express my anger, then, I have to recognize what the particular relationship can bear. Some relationships can bear nothing in the way of expression at all. To deal with our anger in a healthy but realistic way in this kind of relationship is very difficult.

Recently I had several encounters with a person who made me very angry. And I could do nothing about it.

It happened in one of the last classes I had to take for my Ph.D. course work—a class in twentieth-century drama. I wrote a paper, following all the indicated instructions—and the professor refused to read it because it was not exactly what he had in mind. I wrote him an explanatory letter, not calling him a pompous power-hungry sausage (although I sure felt like it!). He smugly told me he would not read the paper so I'd better write another one. I was furious but knew that if I wanted to pass the course I couldn't express my anger to him.

Two days later the same professor failed a close friend of mine in her preliminary oral exam for her Ph.D. because of a departmental power struggle. He had resolved to show his power, come hell or high water. I was furious with this man. He was throwing his weight around at the expense of those less powerful than himself. We find this kind of injustice very difficult to deal with, and we should.

Anger when we are powerless can be hard to handle. I had to remember that my anger in this situation was not sin. Had I (a) not recognized my anger, (b) blasted him with the sentiments I was feeling, or (c) vowed to nurse my anger and never forgive this man, then I would have moved into sin.

When I sat down to rewrite my paper, I got so mad I could hardly write. I sat and prayed for perspective and put on a tape of hymns at full volume. I read a psalm or two because so many of them are written out of David's anger or bewilderment over the seeming victory of the evil-doer. I began to understand that this professor's life was warped; he was involved in these power plays because he was missing something central in his life. I remembered hearing that he had left his job interview with his fingers bloody; he had been so nervous and desperate to get the job he had chewed his fingers. I began to feel sorry for him. I tried to pray for him but this was difficult for me for a few weeks.

When Anger Becomes Bitterness

Bet and her husband Brian had a perfect marriage. They had

become Christians after wild teenage years. They had a baby, worked with street youth and were active in a Bible church that preached a "prosperity" gospel. As young Christians, Bet and Brian took the message of this group to heart, and it affected their view of God. The message was simple: "If I do my part, God will do his part, and everything will always be fine and dandy." The flip side of this, which Bet and Brian hadn't considered, was the question, "What if things are not fine and dandy?"

Bet also learned in this fellowship to equate her husband with the Lord. Brian was the one she looked to; he was the one who acted as Christ to her. Brian decided that he wanted to study medicine so that they could do medical missionary work. They moved to a university town in the Pacific Northwest where Brian could study. Bet loved the idea of becoming a missionary wife. She took a part-time job to support Brian. They found a lively church and got involved.

As Brian was studying for his MCAT, he started having stomach pain. Doctors diagnosed it as stress, but he felt worse and worse. He became anxious and fearful and began to wonder if God had rejected him. Finally, after several months he was diagnosed as having a rare kind of stomach cancer.

Brian had extensive chemotherapy and radiation treatments, and he had to quit his job. Church members provided a house and money for them. People from the church held all-night prayer vigils and brought meals. Still Brian appeared no better. Then Bet discovered that she was pregnant.

After eight months Bet and Brian dropped out of their small support group. Brian hadn't been able to come for months, but Bet told the group that she couldn't keep coming because she was going back to school to become a physical therapist. She might never be able to rely on Brian again to provide meals and a home.

Brian started to improve and then was in total remission. He got a good job. They bought a farm in the foothills of the Cascades. But they don't go to church anymore, and their marriage is rocky.

Bet feels that her husband let her down and God betrayed her. She never wants to be open for that kind of pain again. Bet feels too that people at church let her down. She is angry that no one could adequately tell her where God was when Brian was sick and she was pregnant. Although Brian now appears to be nearly better, Bet will not allow anyone to get close to her. One woman keeps phoning Bet, and Bet says, "Can't she get it through her head that I want to be left alone?"

Bet has chosen to nurse her anger (against God, people and her husband) into bitterness, a bitterness that flavors every part of her life. Not dealt with, her anger has become the central reality in her life. Her bitterness has affected her perspective. Bet cannot see how God has worked through adverse circumstances. She cannot see a hopeful future. She cannot see love in her husband, her friends, or God. Her life has been warped by her bitterness.

Many women have tremendous reasons for anger. Many have been abused, abandoned when their bodies no longer look stunning, barred from the vocation to which they feel called and belittled in public. Many women are tempted to allow their anger to become something cancerous. Ultimately forgiveness is a choice.

Jesus spoke very strongly against bitterness and lack of forgiveness. He told Peter that he must forgive "seventy times seven" and followed with the story of the boss who forgave a servant a huge debt. The servant found a fellow servant who owed him a few bucks and began to threaten him. The boss summoned the servant and punished him for not forgiving as he had been forgiven. Jesus ended his story with these words: "So my heavenly Father will also do to every one of you, if you do not forgive your brother or sister from your heart" (Mt 18:35). When we pray the Lord's prayer we ask that we would be forgiven as we forgive. Even when we have been grossly hurt, we need to recognize our anger and then choose to forgive.

People have sometimes chosen to forgive in the face of the most embittering circumstances. In her extraordinary book about life in a Soviet prison camp, Irina Ratushinskaya had every reason to become bitter. She did become angry. But she writes about her decision not to hate because hatred is so damaging to the one who hates. Hatred spreads its roots, "driving out everything else, and ultimately corrodes and warps your soul." Hatred can become so deeply rooted in us that it actually changes the person who we are until "all that will remain will be a hysterical, maddened and bedeviled husk of the human being that once was." Ratushinskaya writes that she had to think, when she saw a warden who was trying to destroy her, that he might have "children who may grow up to be quite different from him. . . . Or you may feel sincerely sorry for him: no matter how grim your situation, would you swap places with him? Of course not!"[3]

We decide what to do with our anger. First we must recognize the emotion and try to see what our anger is telling us about what is important to us. Then we must decide how to express it, whether we should wait or speak. We may feel tempted to hold onto our anger: "Don't get flabby now . . . keep that anger warm . . . remember what they did to you . . . forgiving would be letting them off easily." There are situations when forgiveness is extraordinarily difficult. But we have the example of

Jesus who forgave his torturers.

Ratushinskaya and other Christians are examples for us; they have gotten angry and found ways to express it without letting it consume them. They have chosen to forgive.

8/BELIEVING DISTORTIONS ABOUT INTIMACY

*S*ex has often been considered to be the really big sin. Dorothy L. Sayers wrote an essay called "The Other Six Deadly Sins" because a young man had told her how surprised he was to hear there were other sins besides sexual ones.[1] Perhaps sex has achieved such notoriety because it is easily distorted by our society. I want to look at two major distortions that lead women into temptation: distortions about intimacy and distortions about sex.

Our society tempts us to believe warped ideas about intimacy and relationships. And the world's temptations have invaded the church. The early adolescent believes that life will be fulfilling when she catches a man; she thinks if she doesn't have a boyfriend, life is hardly worth living. Many Christians buy these ideas even though they contradict the teaching of the New Testament. The New Testament portrays celibacy as a desirable choice or a gift for the greater service of God; most Christians see it as the most calamitous disaster that could befall them.

Distortion 1: A man will make me happy.
"My biology professor thinks I should be pre-med," says Karen, a bright freshman student at a Christian college. "But I'm going to go into nursing. You see, I think it's important that I put my family and husband first."

She looks young, sitting in my office, too young to be so deeply involved with someone. "Are you engaged?"

"Oh, no!" Karen laughs. "I don't even have a boyfriend. Never have. But I believe that the highest calling for a woman is as a wife and mother, and I'm putting that in my career plans." Only eighteen, Karen has carefully learned the catechism taught to her by the world in the church. "What is the highest calling of woman?" Unlike the church catechism that would lead her to reply, "To glorify God and enjoy him forever," Karen has learned the world's version: "To serve a man and make him happy forever."

This worldly idea that Karen has learned so thoroughly has nearly disappeared from secular society. It is now almost exclusively found in certain branches of the church. Most women today do not harbor a dream of being swept away by Prince Charming, according to Ruth Sidel, professor of sociology at Hunter College, New York. From her exhaustive interviews with young women from preteens to mid-twenties, she found that no one thought she could rely on men or society.[2]

Sidel may well be right about young women in society in general, but she obviously wasn't interviewing a group of Christian women. Many Christians suffer from the "white knight syndrome" in which a woman expects a man to fill center stage in her life. It was God's idea that it is not good that a human should live alone, but some Christians warp this romantic ideal: "A man will come and find me and look after me, and I'll make his house nice, and raise nice children for him and cook nice meals for him." This distortion is not only idolatry but also a warping, as bizarre as pornography, of the male/female relationship.

When women believe that finding a man will be the answer to all their dreams and desires, they are swallowing a line the world has told them in countless ways. The most common kind of story that women have read is the "romance" that ends when the woman (usually the attractive young woman) marries. The new "Christian romances" follow this trend, implying that a woman's greatest end is to find a man and make him happy forever.

The "white knight syndrome" doesn't infect only the unmarried. Romance novels offer the promise of passion even to the church-going grandmother. She sits in her living room, with her husband snoring under his newspaper, and fantasizes about a thirty-year-old yachtsman who pulls her to him in his muscular arms and whispers how he cannot live without her. Of all popular paperbacks sold in the United States, forty percent are romance novels.

Who has told women that a only a man will them happy? Pastors and parents and often mothers who never looked at their own lives carefully. Last year I had freshman students read an essay which cites a well-known, oft-repeated statistic that women who work and have families are happier than those who are full-time homemakers. These Christian students, in essays critiquing the article, all denied the accuracy of this statistic. They had been told in no uncertain terms, by conference speakers and pastors, that the only happy woman was the one who stayed home all her life.

When Tracey graduated from high school in Florida, she decided to go to a local Bible college, find a nice young man and become a minister's wife. She studied Christian education and stayed at the college for six years. Then Tracey moved to North Carolina and got a job as a secretary. Still no Mr. Right. She moved back to Florida and got a job teaching in a Christian school, but she only earns $14,000 a year, which means she has to live at home with her mother and stepfather. She is thirty years old. She has few friends because she moves from church to church, always hoping she will meet the right man. She is a victim of the "white knight syndrome."

Women have also been told this fairy tale in stories and movies. But it often resonates with what they'd like to believe. The fairy tale also appeals to women who question their talents and abilities. A woman like Tracey may feel she could not be a very competent school principal, but she's good enough to be someone else's "helpmeet." Men (sometimes unconsciously, to be sure) encourage this distortion. The traditional wife is like the traditional butler in English novels. Who wouldn't want a wife to cook wonderful meals, raise shining offspring, submit to one's every wish, keep the house tidy, iron shirts and provide the necessary sexual outlet in the bedroom?

A woman like Tracey needn't find out what God wants her to do with her life; she can rely on Mr. Right to plan her life for her. If Mr. Right tarries, she will keep seeking the mirage.

The "Pornography" of Romantic Love
In chapter 1 we looked at how women are different from men.

We saw that women tend to emphasize relationships to the exclusion of all else. Emphasizing relationships is not bad, but sometimes we can invest so much in them that they become warped, like reflections in a fun-house mirror. A God-given longing for intimacy with another person may become twisted in us. Pornography is a warping, where the desire for physical satisfaction becomes the whole. Romantic love is another such warping, where a person expects another to be the answer to her life. The romantic image of the damsel swept off her feet by the white knight is no more realistic than the pornographic image of the inexperienced prude turned sex-crazed woman by a macho man.

Romantic love is great. Most marriages in our culture start from the falling-in-love experience, which is not a bad way for a marriage to start. "Romance is a legitimate and important early stage of love. The powerful attraction we feel for one another fuels the movement toward commitment, encouraging us to be open to the risks and possibilities that marriage will bring."[3]

Scott Peck in *The Road Less Traveled* points out that this romantic stage passes, as the lovers begin to see that their loved one is different from themselves. Peck sees this as the time for real love to begin, when romantic infatuation runs out.[4] Evelyn and James Weatherhead put it this way: "Marriage matures as love becomes an active choice. This realization moves us beyond the exhilarating but largely passive experience of 'falling in love' toward love as a cultivated and chosen commitment. . . . The challenge is not to keep on loving the person we thought we were marrying, but to love the person we did marry!"[5]

The "end" of the romantic ideal can be a tremendous stress for the Christian woman, such a stress that she cannot face it.

For her it is the end of a calling, a profession, a ministry, as well as the end of a dream. She may crack, as we saw Jill do in our introduction, when she sees that her white knight is not what she expected. She may sink into bitterness, as Bet did, when her white knight (for any reason) can no longer protect and be everything to her.

A single woman may have a faraway white knight; in the here-and-now she longs for the perfect man, the one who will fulfill her every need.

I knew it was meant to be. Dan's room number in the Sherwood Forest student apartments was 814. The address of the house where I lived with five women students was 814 First Street. Dan invited me to go to the college Highland fest with him; I felt proud to watch the bagpipers with him since he was Scottish. We stood on the deck looking out over Puget Sound, the reels wafting out to us. He put his arm around me, and I knew this was the guy for me.

Dan was tall and slender. He had dark curly hair, an impish face, blue eyes that sparkled. He seemed very childlike to me; he would get wildly enthusiastic about good food, hiking, biking, snow, sailing. He also had a lovely tenor voice; I remember him singing "Just a Closer Walk with Thee" with my old pal Ed.

When I think about the intensity of this relationship, which lasted only six or eight months and devastated me when it ended, I think much of it was the idealism that I brought to the relationship. I'd been involved with lots of other men, but this was my first relationship since I'd become a Christian. I felt as if I loved Dan with a depth of love that I'd never known before.

Dan became the answer to my deepest desires and (perhaps more important) to the Christian teaching on relationships that I was receiving. Our life together would be wonderful. I would live for him. I didn't need to choose a major. I didn't need to plan a career. Our children would be cute little "Dans." What more could a woman want?

In the falling-in-love experience, the woman is a passive and emotional recipient of male attention. The romantic scenario portrays the male hero who rescues and then possesses the waiting damsel in distress. He is the active agent and she is the passive cooperator. This romantic experience, plus Christian teaching that emphasizes the passive nature of the woman's part in the sexual relationship, sets a woman up to be unaware of herself in marriage. She assumes that if she is sweet and cooperative to her man, she will be happy and satisfied. Reality may bring terrible emotional upheaval.

Distortion 2: Celibacy is the worst thing for a woman.
Our culture tells a woman that without a man she is nothing. Think even of our vocabulary: an unmarried man is a bachelor and that implies fun. An unmarried woman is a spinster or an old maid, someone left on the shelf, helpless, weak and impossibly frustrated.

This need to be with someone is exploited by dating services, commonly known as the "agony industry." The dating service industry had just under a thousand businesses nationwide in 1989 and "grosses between 100-300 million dollars a year."[6]

The "agony industry" is even exploited by Christian publishers. The world has clearly invaded the church; we can see this in a book published in 1989 instructing women in how to "catch a man." The author, using the pseudonym Jennifer Logan, was understandably too embarrassed to use her real name but Word Publishing sports its insignia on the spine of the book. The title *Not Just Any Man: A Guide to Finding Mr. Right* should be changed to *As Long As It's Wearing Pants: How to Not Get Left on the Shelf.*

Jennifer Logan points out that women's biological clocks tick faster than men's. A woman cannot afford to wait; she needs to get busy and find a man. A man wants to be needed; he wants a woman who will depend on him, not a woman who is competent or intelligent because it might make him feel threatened: "Downplay your job and accomplishments everywhere but on your resume." A woman who is too together will scare men off. "You're in the sales business," Logan writes, "presenting yourself to the world as a woman who would like to marry a special man."[7] What else could a person want?

Logan is very practical. She found through surveys that men prefer women with long, blonde hair; she warns, "Don't ever go out in public with even one nail chipped or peeling."[8] Women need to be careful about the kind of jewelry they wear because men get confused by rings and might think you're married or engaged. Even pictures of children on your desk at work might confuse the eligible bachelor.

A woman needs to give a man "blue ribbons." To a man in the office, she might say, "I really think you are the best salesman in the company." At church, of course, things are a little different. She might "comment on how much more perceptive he is than others or how much more he's thought through his beliefs than other men." Honesty is not really an issue: "Of course you should base your comparison on some supporting evidence, but don't be too literal."[9]

One great way to catch a man is through borrowing a neighbor's child and taking him or her to a public place. There the woman can skip, giggle, roll down hills (because childlike behavior attracts a man); and when she has a chance she can tell the man that this is not her child, but she loves children, "quickly establishing availability."[10] Logan suggests other ways to catch this man: going into a male-dominated field like UPS, visiting different churches, attending graduate school and hanging out in airport lounges flirting with bored business travelers (though of course at this point the woman needs to dress the part with a suit and briefcase, even if she's never flown in her life). Photography and auto clubs or car showrooms are also good bets.

When the Christian woman is out to find Mr. Right, she can take some props. Logan suggests any book by C. S. Lewis, a recent copy of *Sports Illustrated* ("Not the swimsuit issue, unless you have a figure as good as the cover model's"), *The Wall Street Journal,* a T-shirt with a school name or fun location. "Wear one with the name of a Christian school or organization if you want to narrow the field to Christian men. Don't wear a T-shirt with a cutesy or feminist slogan."[11] "Take a hat, a dog, a camera, a tennis or racquetball racquet (and put on your tennis dress if you have good legs), fun sunglasses and a crazy button that says nothing political, feminist, or combative."[12] Logan occasionally reminds her readers how effective her methods are by telling them the results: poor, lonely Christian women end up "married with three children."

That a Christian writer and publisher would be willing to exploit desperate and powerless people is remarkable but understandable. Why? Because the church has taught that a woman is nothing without a man. We invest more faith in romance than we do in God. There are stories in the early church of women longing to be free to follow Christ, of facing martyrdom in order not to be tied down by marriage. Today the chief end of a woman is to find a man and make him happy forever.

When we describe an unmarried person we may say, "Well, she's single." Being single is her dominant characteristic. One woman writes:

"I'm always surprised when I realize people think of me as

single. It's true that I am not married and that I live alone. . . . 'Being single' is as little a part of my sense of myself as 'having blue eyes'; as a statement of fact, it's accurate enough, but it has little to do with who I am."[13] Singleness is in fact the way we are born: it is our natural state. We might as well call marriage a state of "unsingleness."[14]

"Singleness" for a woman implies rejection and lack of choice, especially since our society has traditionally identified a woman's relational, nurturing qualities as her most important ones. And if the single woman feels bad about her state, she is more likely to become involved in unhealthy relationships, or to be drawn to marry someone who will not walk with her in a life of faith. This is one of the greatest temptations a woman will face.

Beth became a Christian, after a long struggle, two months before her wedding date. Her fiance, Wendell, didn't want her to attend church or to hang around with Christians.

Beth's Christian friends counseled her not to marry Wendell, or at least to wait awhile. But Beth was thirty-six and felt tremendous pressure to "normalize" by marriage. She went ahead with it.

Six months later, I sat in bed after midnight one night as my husband tried to counsel Wendell on the phone. From my side of the bed I could hear through the phone the occasional smashing of glass. As Wendell talked to my husband, Beth was smashing the windows of their house with a cricket bat. Beth and Wendell's marriage struggled along for a few more months before he disappeared. She had succumbed to the world's tempting lie: "you ain't nothin' without a man."

Women have been told that their highest calling is as a good wife and mother. "Because marriage and motherhood have been so widely identified as a woman's true vocation, single women are often seen as only half-women."[15] The Protestant church eliminated celibacy with medieval monasticism, but many women with effective ministries in recent years have been single.[16] Motherhood may be a high calling indeed, but if it is the ultimate call, single women are denied companionship, legitimacy and access to the highest calling.

We can see how successful the world has been at marketing its product to the church, when we see how the church underlines family and marriage as the ultimate good and forgets the witness of Scripture. Few churches see celibacy as a viable option; instead they make singleness more difficult for Christian women. Many churches have sections in their bulletins or monthly publications celebrating and congratulating couples on their engagements, their weddings, their babies. They fuss over Mother's Day. The engaged woman or the one who is having a baby gets showers and presents. The single woman who is attempting to live a celibate life, in spite of all the pressures from the media, society, family and the church, struggles on. No one celebrates her.

The apostle Paul celebrated singleness and Jesus referred to the disciples as closer than family. Paul suggests to Christians in 1 Corinthians that they may be more effective Christians if they are unmarried; he treats this as a healthy and holy state for Christians (1 Cor 7:36). Unfortunately, we have swallowed the world's story, hook, line and sinker.

How should the Christian single respond? We need to be honest with God if we feel he has let us down. My psychologist friend tells me that many of her clients are Christian women who feel unworthy without a man. Because they are not married, they feel that they are missing out on life's fullest and as women they feel powerless; women simply do not ask men to marry them. So although a woman who wants to marry may try

to meet people and may pray fervently, she is essentially helpless and passive. She may well be mad at God. But she doesn't
know she can be mad at God, so it comes out in depression and
helplessness. God (as we see in the Psalms) can handle our
anger. We can tell God if we're angry with him.

The Christian single needs to move out of guilt. In her article
"The Desires of Thine Heart," Evelyn Bence reflects on the
single life. She talks about the assurances from her grandmother and her brother that God would fulfill her heart's desire, and
how she was disappointed when God didn't come through.

She talks about learning to recognize her feelings and about
cutting free from the spiral of guilt that comes from not being
content with Jesus and still longing for a man. Bence sees some
of this desperate desire for intimacy as a result of the fall, and
as with other effects of the fall (pain in childbirth for instance)
the Christian should not feel guilty for experiencing it. She
suggests that the single woman define the source of discontent
and get rid of unnecessary guilt, doing the "emotional equivalent of a pregnant woman's breathing exercises. . . . Fighting
against legitimate pain . . . makes it worse, the embracing of it
. . . mysteriously breaks its controlling power over us and makes
us more conscious of God's spiritual and sustaining presence."[17]

Although God instituted marriage, he didn't make a perfect
person who would fulfill our every need and then hide him
under a bush somewhere. Although God saw that Adam and
Eve needed each other, they were obviously not the answer to
each other's problems, or else we'd still be in the garden. I
know from my experience that marriage can be an environment where our lives are enriched, where personal growth is
fostered, where we can have some good laughs, sustain each
other's values, hide when the children seem overwhelming. But

marriage will not make me whole. Only God can do that.

The temptation for us to settle for the world's distortions, to expect someone to come along and make us happy, to find our center outside of God, is powerful. Satan will encourage women to settle for less than the best. We need to know ourselves, identify the power of the world's influence on us, and seek God's good plan for our individual lives and his pattern for nourishing relationships within the Christian community.

9/BELIEVING DISTORTIONS ABOUT SEX

*W*hen *I was in junior high, a cellist in the sixth grade orchestra* threw a party. Greg insisted that his parents had promised that they would stay upstairs while the party went on in the paneled rec room in the basement. Greg's girlfriend, a violinist named Marcia, helped him pair up the orchestra members who would come to the party. I was paired with Eric. During orchestra practice I would sometimes find Eric staring at me.

The night of the party arrived. We played ping-pong, drank pop and ate hot dogs. Then Marcia and Greg sat on a couch and "made out." After a brief demonstration, Marcia pulled away from Greg and said, "You try it," to the other eight of us.

"It's great," Greg agreed. I was supposed to "make out" with Eric, who didn't even play the viola very well. I looked at him and then phoned my mom. "I don't feel so good, Mom. Will you come and get me?"

It was two years later that I discovered my sexual desires and realized that I had something that could make me attractive to members of the opposite sex. I met Randy just after school started in September, and we spent evenings playing pool in his garage, three houses down from ours. One evening he put his pool cue in the rack and turned to me. He put his arms around me and kissed me, pressing his body against mine. Suddenly, I understood what the big deal was with sex. I also recognized that simply being female gave me a certain power over someone like Randy. I liked that.

Adolescent Sexuality

Nearly twenty-five years later, a ten-year-old girl named Sammie lives around the corner from us. She brags about the R-rated movies she has seen and talks about watching the Playboy cable channel when her father is passed-out, drunk. She dyes her hair blonde and dresses to show off her body that is just beginning to develop. When my thirteen-year-old son is home, she sits provocatively on our front steps, talking to my seven-year-old daughter, telling her how cute her older brother is. Sammie's home has provided her with no security, no firm foundation from which to encounter life, but she knows the beginnings of sexual urgings. And she thinks that sex may provide a key to her finding some power in her life.

Sex can be overwhelming for adolescents; it can excite and even threaten them as nothing else can. "Maturing into adult life, we gradually befriend sex—learning to appreciate its power, to savor its delights, to see through some of its illusions. We make decisions that integrate sexual activity in our lives in ways that are consistent with our deepest values."[1] But our society urges "us to linger too long in adolescence. Our society exalts sex as the peak experience and primary focus of life."[2] We cooperate with the world's temptation to linger by seeing movies or reading novels that promote unhealthy sexual activity and make fidelity or abstinence more difficult. The world would like us all to remain in this breathless, selfish stage of sexuality; it would like all of us to stick at the maturity level of my turned-on ten-year-old neighbor Sammie.

The Power of Sexuality

What are we to make of the strong sexual desires and the powerful hold that sexuality can have on our lives? Christian theologians and counselors affirm that our sexuality is a good gift from God, invented by God to be used within certain boundaries. The Song of Solomon is a celebration of married sexual joy. Jesus reminded those who were listening to him that in the marriage union, the couple "are no longer two, but one flesh" (Mt 19:6). In the Garden of Eden "the man and his wife were both naked, and were not ashamed" (Gen 2:25).

Lewis Smedes comments that "there are two situations in which people feel no shame. The first is in a state of wholeness. The other is in a state of illusion."[3] God's intention for sexuality and the sexual reality that we live in can seem miles apart, as far apart as wholeness and illusion. Why? Because the world, the flesh and the devil delight (as usual) to distort a good gift from God; they twist it to offer us temptations. We know the temptation to remain in an adolescent sexuality that is self-consumed and never satisfied; we know the temptation to use our sexuality as power.

If sexuality is a good gift from God but has been distorted to wreak havoc in our lives, how should we respond? We must identify the distortions and understand the temptations they present.

Distortion 1: Sexuality is bad.
For hundreds of years women were not allowed a legitimate sexuality. Women, as we have seen in chapter two, were regarded as temptresses who would lead men astray. This was often encouraged by a double standard. A man wanted a woman who was sexually passionate, so he kept a mistress or visited a prostitute who fulfilled this role. A man also wanted a woman who was sexually pure. He, as lord of the manor, needed to know that the child his wife bore was his heir and not some bastard, so his wife became the other part of the man's double sex life. She was pure and would bear and raise his children, unlike his mistress who was seductive, hidden and fun.

Often a woman has felt that she had to make a choice in coming to terms with her sexuality. Would she be the pure woman who indulged in the sexual act with her husband only for procreative purposes, or would she be the woman who relished her sexuality and was ostracized by proper society? Saint or whore? Women felt that they had to choose.

This distortion that sexuality is bad, and that a woman must choose whether to be whore or saint, has been popularized by images like that of the Virgin Mary. At the retreat house that I visit once a month, she stands in a little alcove at the top of the stairs, robed in pastel green and rose, her head veiled, her eyes focused not on the baby she holds or the viewer but down on something near her right foot. She looks passive and helpless. She is one of many statues and pictures of the Virgin Mary, and many women feel that as an ideal presented to them to emulate, she has not been helpful. She is ever virgin (sexless) and yet ever mother (available for the procreation of the species). Ever virgin, ever mother: some would say this is the worst of all possible worlds!

Where did such a view come from? We can lay some blame at the feet of early church fathers like St. Augustine. He wrote of "the shame which attends all sexual intercourse" in his very influential *City of God*.[4] Some people suggest that Augustine's teaching on sexuality was a reaction to his pre-Christian promiscuity. After his conversion he couldn't separate the ideas of intimacy and lust. He assumed that all intimacy was like his previous wild lustful passions.[5] Whatever Augustine's problem, his thinking has been duplicated by others in the church. Medieval theologians taught that the Holy Spirit would not remain present when a couple had intercourse. They urged the faithful to abstain on certain days of the week and during Lent.

Distortion 2: Women don't have problems with "classic" lust.
"Why have I been given the impression ever since I became a Christian that sex and lust are not a problem for women?" says Emily, the wife of a minister. "I regularly struggle with strong sexual feelings for men other than my husband. I fantasize about them.

"I also avoid them," Emily continued. "When I have a crush on someone, I just don't go anywhere that he might be. I wouldn't dream of getting myself into a compromising situation with a man. But talks and books and sermons and talk shows make it sound as if Christian women, or maybe particularly wives, don't struggle with this. When the Bible talks about our 'unruly passions' that need to be controlled, I know just what it means" (Rom 7:5; Col 3:5; Gal 5:24; Tit 2:12, 3:13).

The double standard is still alive and well today. It tells us that women's sex drives are weak, while men's are strong. For

centuries an unchaste man was regarded as normal, an unchaste woman as a whore; when a woman was raped, people
assumed that she had asked for it. The sexual double standard
implies that "good girls don't, but boys will be boys." A politi-
cian who got into trouble over some sexual impropriety com-
mented, "For a few years there, I was very much the red-
blooded American male." In other words, it's okay to be sexually active if you are a man; boys will be boys.

Think back to Jill and her slide into adultery. It was classic
lust that finally put her over the edge. She didn't know that as
a woman she could be capable of such intense passion. Jill had
little awareness of the strength of her sexual drives or how to
handle them. Her lack of self-knowledge, combined with her
poor self-image, was disastrous to her.

Bonnie is a forty-one-year-old editor with a large multi-na-
tional corporation. She leads a Bible study group and has many
friends. She has dated on and off but hasn't met a man whom
she would like to marry. She struggles to cope with her sexuality.

"When I was in college I met a man who really set me on
fire sexually. As a Christian I knew that intercourse was out. But
I could just see him across a room and begin to feel aroused."

Bonnie thought her sexual feelings were weird, that she was
alone in them. She figured "good Christian women" didn't feel
attracted sexually to men. "I think the thing that bothers me
most is the fact that I've never been able to put my strong sexual
fantasies together with feelings of love and attachment. So they
feel dirty. But they're still there. And I don't know what to do
about them. I sometimes wonder if it is easier for people who
were sexually active before they had a dramatic conversion. At
least they know what they're missing. I'm afraid I'll go to the
grave without ever knowing what it's like to be loved by a man.

I know—as a Christian I'm supposed to be glad that I am still a virgin. But I don't know if I really am happy about it or not."

Bonnie's ambivalence may stem from the fact that Christian women don't talk about their sexual feelings. If Bonnie were a man who felt overwhelmed by sexual desires, she would be considered normal. Christian women have been told that they don't have feelings like that. This may be largely because Christian women learn about sex from a male perspective. Men describe their own sexual experience for themselves, and then go on to tell women what *their* sexual feelings will (or ought to) be like.

Distortion 3: Sex is a male need.
Women have learned to think about their sexuality primarily as it derives from male sexuality. Even the words we use to talk about sex assume a male perspective. The word *foreplay* assumes that what is often the most satisfying part of sex for a woman is only a preliminary to the important part, penetration, writes Dale Spender. She suggests that *enclosure* might better express a feminine perspective of the sex act.[6]

Seminary textbooks teach future pastors about marriage counseling. Here's what one of the books advises men: "A wife should know the difference between the sexual needs of the male and female. Generally a husband is more physical in his needs and response, whereas a wife is more emotional in her needs and response. The husband can become sexually aroused quickly and tends to be more sexually assertive, sometimes desiring sexual intercourse more frequently than his wife."[7] Further down the page, these three experts suggest this to a woman: "Don't be unattractive in bed. Some wives go to bed at night in dingy flannel pajamas, or slathered with greasy face creams."[8] This advice assumes a totally male perspective.

Willard Harley suggests, in *His Needs, Her Needs: Building an Affair-Proof Marriage,* that men need the following from their spouses: sexual fulfillment, recreational companionship (someone to do sports activities with), an attractive spouse, domestic support (a quiet and well-ordered home) and admiration. What does a woman need from her husband? Harley answers: affection, conversation, honesty and openness, financial support and family commitment. In his chapter "The First Thing He Can't Do Without: Sexual Fulfillment" he gives Harley's First Corollary: "The typical wife doesn't understand her husband's deep need for sex any more than the typical husband understands his wife's deep need for affection."[9] Once again, sex from a male perspective.

Textbooks and popular Christian marriage books portray women in a passive role in sex. Although to her man physical satisfaction is important, a woman will find her satisfaction in a nice warm bed, the secure roof overhead and the thought of the children nestled all snug in their beds.

June belonged to a quilting group in her church in Pittsburgh. The women brought patchwork patterns, swapped them and then talked as they quilted. Often they closed their time in prayer. One week the subject of temptation came up. They went around the circle, and each woman shared an area with which she struggled. "I find the latest fashions really appeal to me, and I want to go and buy them." "I spend too much on home decorating, like those new blinds I ordered last week." "I find it hard to get into a regular quiet time routine."

It was June's turn. "I've never told anybody this before, but I really struggle with lust. I mean really struggle. It's not that I don't love my husband, but when I look at my sixteen-year-old's music teacher, I am overcome with desire. I am incredibly physically and emotionally attracted to him."

There was a silence. The woman next to her broke in, "I sometimes get irritated at my mother-in-law." June felt as if she was very strange to struggle with lust. As she packed her quilting into her bag, she felt very much alone.

That evening June phoned a friend in the group. "I really felt dumb about this afternoon," she said. "I guess I misjudged the situation; I wanted to share that with someone and it seemed like the time. But I guess I embarrassed everyone, including myself. I just wanted to tell someone what a fool I felt."

June's friend paused. "I'm glad you were so honest," she said. "Since this afternoon, my phone's been ringing. Two different women told me that they had been considering getting into adulterous affairs, but that because of your honesty, they have resolved not to."

Most Christian women assume that their sexual life after marriage will be fulfilling. So united will they be—soul, mind and body—with their spouse, that sex will be wonderful. If a woman feels strong sexual stirrings that are not satisfied in her marriage, they may simply "not compute." Her dissatisfaction in her marital sex may spark guilt; she will think, "Well, he's really so nice to me, and the children are wonderful; so I guess it doesn't really matter. There's nothing wrong with our sex life."

The problem is that good sex in marriage involves being in touch with myself, my feelings and what arouses me. As a hangover from distortion number one (sex is bad), many women were raised with shameful feelings about their body parts and are really not altogether sure what makes them tick. Add to that distortion number two, which encourages women to think of sex as designed primarily for the physical satisfaction of the man, and you have a potentially explosive situation. We saw this in Jill's experience: when women are out of touch with their sexual feelings they are very vulnerable to sudden sexual temptation. We need to recognize the fact that we are sexual beings who have sexual feelings.

Distortion 4: A happy marriage means fulfilling sexual intimacy. Our society has encouraged an inequality in marriage that suggests that one partner exists (in any one of a number of ways) for the convenience of the other. This often happens domestically, where one partner does most of the housework, but it can also happen sexually, where one partner finds sexual satisfaction and the other learns to "get by." Christian women can easily become sex objects, settling for being an answer to their husband's sexual needs. Often women who are experiencing marital dissatisfaction blame themselves. They wonder if they are giving enough and giving implies a kind of passivity.

Many Christian women are not even sure how to think about their sexuality, let alone talk about it. They have assumed that their sexual satisfaction is derivative—what more satisfaction could she want than that he be satisfied? Women can live for years, rising above their bodily appetites by finding satisfaction in their children, a kiss from hubby when he comes in from the office, or the occasional three-minute love-making session before he drifts off to sleep.

If a woman suddenly recognizes strong sexual feelings that are not being met in her marriage, it may affect other aspects of her marriage or she may be tempted to find sexual satisfaction elsewhere.

Ann and Clive met when he was finishing his degree as an architect and she was completing an M.A. in journalism. They married eight months later. She enjoyed homemaking, cooking and raising the kids. She felt their sexual life was pretty good, certainly nothing to complain about, although the interruptions of four pregnancies, four rounds of breastfeeding and sleepless nights didn't help. For a year or two she worried about another pregnancy. When they made love, Ann pretended everything was fine. Maybe she thought everything was fine.

A couple of years ago she went back to school to take some classes. She came across a writer who suggested that very few women really know their bodies, really know what makes them sexual beings. She recognized that this was true for her. She realized that she had assumed as she and Clive had more sexual experience together, she would find more sexual satisfaction. She saw that she'd been giving Clive the impression that their sex life was fine. Ann realized that her whole married life could be like this: not unhappy but not really working at her sexual life, not being as honest as she might be, not really finding out what brought her more than occasional sexual satisfaction.

Ann felt scared. Her discovery of strong sexual feelings made her feel almost dizzy. The ground seemed to shake beneath her; she wondered if she was the woman she thought she was. Ann realized that if she were a man, all of this would sound ridiculous. It was because she was female, married and Christian that it seemed so strange.

Ann knew that to be out of touch with one area of herself, like her sexuality, put her in a dangerous position. How would she handle it if Clive was away and she was suddenly put in a tempting situation? She didn't want to find out.

Ann handled her situation well. She recognized her strong sexual feelings. And she talked to Clive about them. "I took Clive out to dinner and told him I needed to talk to him about something. Somehow this was one of the hardest things I'd ever done. I said to him, 'Clive, this is hard for me to tell you but I've decided I'm not getting as much satisfaction in our sex life as I'd like. I've really sublimated all this, and I'm not willing to any longer. So let's try a reversal. How would you feel if for a month we organized our love-making sessions for my satisfaction, and your satisfaction will be an extra bonus, if it happens?' "

He was obviously a little taken aback, but he agreed. She says that the results have been terrific for them both. Ann and Clive have confirmed what Dr. Norman Lobenz writes, "There is no better safeguard against infidelity than a vital, interesting marriage."[10]

Two years later when Ann reflected on this time, she realized that what made it hardest was the fact that she felt that there was no one she could talk to. How could she as a happily married woman say to a friend as she buttered a bran muffin, "Say, how often do you have orgasms?" When she was exploring some new, strong sexual feelings, she felt impossibly isolated, because there seemed to be no one with whom she could discuss her sexuality.

When we don't talk about things that are on our minds, we tend to become obsessed with them. And when people don't really talk about their feelings, they tend to get false impressions of each other's lives. For the single woman or the woman questioning her sex life, all the couples in the pews around her seem to be the epitome of wedded bliss. She doesn't know that Don and Linda have argued for weeks about money, or that Frank and Sara are having sexual difficulties to the point that they haven't had sex in six months. Sharing with others can help us get perspective on our lives, to get outside what the world has told us.

We shouldn't be surprised that sex raises as many temptations as it does for Christian women. As Christian women we are not encouraged to recognize our sexual feelings. Then we are barraged by media that promote adolescent sex. An active sexual life is the norm in ads, sitcoms, soap operas and movies. Gothic novels move to their culmination when the active, wealthy hero gets the heroine to succumb. Not only is raw sex portrayed, but fulfillment through sex seems to be easily achieved. Despite medical studies to the contrary, the media portrays multiple, simultaneous orgasms (between stars with perfect bodies) as the norm.

These distortions leave us unprepared to cope with the power of sexual feelings. We feel that we shouldn't have powerful sexual feelings. When we are overwhelmed by them, we are tempted to find "free sex," sex that doesn't require the costly commitment that the New Testament equates with becoming one flesh.

Distortion 5: There is free sex.

Pat lived with a man for eight years before she became a Christian. Her family background had been torn by alcoholism, and she was twenty-one when she met Ben. Pat learned an important lesson from her sexual involvement with this man: there is no such thing as "free sex." When she talked to me about her years of trying to get free from this live-in relationship, she described the break-up as extremely traumatic, almost like a divorce.

"You know, I knew within the first year, maybe earlier, probably that first summer, that my relationship with Ben wasn't going to work out. We weren't good for each other. But we were so entangled that it took me another seven years to pull my way out of it. I was stuck. I've resolved never to get physically involved with someone outside marriage again."

Jesus had dealings during his earthly ministry with several women who had used their sexuality to try to find more self-worth, more power. Jesus' response to the promiscuous woman at the well was to tell her how she could find "living water" that would satisfy her deepest thirst. Jesus delivered Mary Magdalene and became her friend. With the woman taken in adultery, Jesus sent her condemners away and told her to "go and sin no more."

Sex is a binding force for a woman. At the wrong time, or with the wrong man, it puts her in bondage. Pat is a living testimony to the truth of the biblical view of sex. Premarital sex is wrong, not because sex is evil, but because it is so powerful. As Evelyn and James Weatherhead point out, it is hard to keep sex casual because it brings with it so much more.[12] Intercourse affects the perspective of the couple involved. It may lead to wasted years or even wasted lives.

10/GETTING STUCK
IN OUR
DISSATISFACTION

I *was in California visiting Kris who longs to be married. Saturday* evening she and I talked in her apartment. She told me, tears running down her cheeks, "You know, I really find it hard not to envy you your husband, and your family, your home. I'm nearly forty and I feel incomplete. I don't know what I've done wrong, and sometimes I think that I've been obedient to my Christian faith, and this is how I get repaid. But this feeling inside, of wanting something so badly and seeing other people who take it for granted . . . sometimes it eats me up."

The next morning Kris and I sat in church together. The reading was from 1 Peter 2:1, "Rid yourselves, therefore, of envy." Kris turned to me and rolled her eyes. "If only it were that easy," she fumed. "If I could just take my envy and put it away in a cupboard or maybe stick it in one of those rental storage places. Didn't Peter know that no one *wants* envy? No one chooses to be envious."

Envy is an unattractive temptation. At least greed, lust and gluttony offer some tangible (though fleeting) pleasures before the guilt sets in! Envy seems to be only negative, only painful, only designed to make us feel bad and guilty. Envy can be a major problem for many women, and it can fill us with such remorse that we are incapacitated by our feelings.

Envy is often crippling for women—the frustrated single, the envious wife of the adulterous husband, the woman who envies the children or grandchildren of another. When we think of envy, we associate it more with women than men. "If only my children had really listened to me, they would be college graduates like yours." "If only I could have a baby." "She didn't deserve the promotion (or scholarship) as much as I did."

Why should envy be more of a problem for women than men? Maybe because we have had fewer opportunities to figure out what we really want, fewer opportunities to make plans to get what we want. Women have been the watchers and waiters: "Will a man come along who will ask me to marry him?" "Will my husband (or son) come home from the war?" "Will I get pregnant this month?" "When will the baby come?" Because in many situations we have been not the doers but the waiters and watchers, we are tempted to envy those who have what we so desperately want.

What, according to the Bible, should we do about the problem of envy? The Bible lists envy with other temptations (Mk 7:22; Rom 1:29; Gal 5:21; Tit 3:13; Jas 3:14). Paul writes that "love is not envious" (1 Cor 13:4) and in Galatians he lists envy with the works of the flesh. But solutions to envy are few. Several proverbs suggest that we shouldn't do it (Prov 23:17) and, as we have noted, Peter tells Christians to put away envy.

Envy often springs from a woman's sense of helplessness, her sense of being a victim of circumstances. How can we put away envy when we never invited it in the first place? How can we deal with that terrible feeling that seems to rise from the center of our soul with great destructive power? Ignoring envy doesn't work. If we push away our envy without looking at what it's telling us about ourselves, it will certainly raise its head again.

Recognizing Our Envy

First we must recognize envy in our lives. Envy is not one shade of green; it ranges across a continuum from wanting to harm another through self-loathing and resentment to covetousness. Sometimes envy can be closely related to admiration for another and even emulation of that person.[1] But envy also has a painful and destructive force; it is then that it seems to tear at our lives.

What are signs of envy in our lives? See if these sound familiar:

1. Do I feel pain because of another person's success?

2. Do I compare myself with someone who is more successful and feel bad about his or her success?

3. Do I feel that I deserve what I envy?

4. Do I find myself wanting to put down successful people by gossiping about them or hurting them?

5. Do I avoid seeing other people's successes?

6. Do I find myself wanting to gain from other people's losses?[2]

Many different things may cause us to envy. Perhaps a close

friend has a baby when we are childless, perhaps our neighbor buys a cabin at the lake when we are struggling to make mortgage payments, perhaps our college roommate meets the man of her dreams while we are dateless.

We may not know we are envious until we find ourselves gossiping about someone. (When we think of gossip, we think of women, perhaps because of strong cultural norms against women succeeding.) "Well, they're rolling in cash, they can afford it; still you wonder where they got it, don't you?" "Their kids seem fine now, but you can be sure that all that private schooling breeds snobs in the end!"

Other times our envy surfaces as a surprising feeling. A friend moves into a new role, and I realize that I'm feeling very strange about it. On reflection I recognize the feelings as envy compounded by guilt about the envy. Envy can cause tremendous conflict between friends.

A very close friend and I were mothers together for years, taking our children on trips to the park together, baking cookies with them, making playdough. Then the time came when I felt I should return to school and start teaching. My move caused serious conflicts in our relationship. We found it difficult to be together. She began to feel that I would no longer care about our old mutual interests. If I spoke about a class I was teaching or a course I was taking, I would realize that I was upsetting her and stop.

Role change often strains a friendship, and the root of this conflict is envy. We feel more comfortable if we all stay the same, if no one in our group of friends decides to do something different, if no one starts to see new possibilities. Because we as women have lacked a broad range of life choices, we may feel threatened when someone we know moves into a new field or part of life, leaving us behind. This is envy.

My friend may have envied my new horizons, my job, my relative independence. I envied my friend's life that looked to me like the good old days when I had time to bake bread. I envied her for not having to help earn money for the family.

Learning from Our Envy

Feelings of envy usually just appear; we seldom decide, "Sure, I'll go for it! Envy, here I come!" But after we recognize envy in our lives, we need to stop and ask why it is there. If we can find envy's roots, we will find it saying something important about our lives. Then we can start to "put away envy."

Obviously my friend and I had some serious work to do along this line. We had to talk this situation out together and clarify our conflict.

We may learn several things by looking at the roots of envy.

Envy Shows Us What We Really Want

Envy can be an emotional indicator helping us to get in touch with what we really think. When we feel envious and before we start to feel guilty, we should ask ourselves, "What is this envy telling me about what I truly want?"

A week after my conversation with Kris in church, I walked along with my husband and the dog on the first springlike evening of the year.

"You know, Ernie," I said, "I've experienced envy, but I'm not sure I've experienced envy like Kris's; she told me that her envy sometimes seems to be eating her up. Is it just because I'm very fortunate . . . you know, I have been blessed with two legs that work fine and a family that hasn't all left me yet?"

"When have you felt envious?" Ernie asked.

"Okay. I used to feel really envious when I was driving the carpool and had to drop off Billy. When I took him into his house, the cleaning person had just been there and the house shone, the floors gleamed; and I knew I was going home to a dirty house and I didn't feel like doing housework. And I couldn't afford to have someone to clean but Beth could because she worked full-time outside the home, and I didn't. Though I'd chosen not to at that point. Still, I felt *green*."

"So, what did you do about it?" Ernie asked as the dog pulled us along the sidewalk.

"Now that I think about it, I really hated that feeling of envy. It made me feel powerless, so I tried to figure out what I could do about it. I decided that I resented the hours spent rounding up kids for the car pool and dropping them off all over creation, so I decided they could take the city bus the next year. And I decided that I was probably a little bored since the kids were in school so I got a part-time job and used some of the money to hire a student to clean every couple of weeks.

"But that was easy; those were things I could do something about."

We passed a lilac bush that was just coming into blossom. "When else have you felt envious?"

"When people go on trips to Europe and come back talking about the museums they have taken their children to, I feel a bit green. I'd love to take the kids to Europe.

"But," I continued, "that's one of the things about envy. I see the trip but I forget the long hours they work, even on the first perfect spring day. I also forget that they've made other choices about priorities, choices that we wouldn't have made. My envy of others' travel doesn't go away. I still feel a bit envious, but when I stop to think about the choices I have made and the other things I have, then I don't feel quite so much like a victim. I think maybe we see one part of people's lives and envy that— and forget the rest that we don't envy at all."

We must look clearly at what our envy tells us about our lives. It offers us an opportunity to question what's really important to us. Sometimes we will look at our envy and be able to act on it, as I did concerning a cleaning person. Sometimes we will look at our envy and see how it indicates choices we've made; nothing will be different, but we will at least have a sense of not being a victim of circumstances. Other times, our envy indicates misplaced values.

When I find myself envying another writer her publishing success, I may conclude that I should invest more of my time in my writing. But it may also make me realize that I'm longing for external successes, that I'm too concerned with what others think, and that I need to spend more time with God and find my center in him. My envy is like a smoke detector; I need to check and see what it's telling me about what I really care about; some of those values may need to be changed.

Sometimes our envy indicates a desperate pain about a situation we can't change. The ongoing envy-pain for the childless couple encountering someone with a new baby may seem overwhelming. It may indicate to them that they should seriously pursue adoption. For my single friend, her ongoing envy may be an indication to her that she still wants to be married more than she thought and that this is an area that she needs to work to come to terms with. She may need to talk to a counselor and explore some of the emotional complications that underlie her need. She may find that she needs to change her lifestyle so that she can establish long-term friendships to fulfill her need for intimacy. We need to ask ourselves what our envy means in terms of what we want.

Envy Shows Us We've Been Afraid to Want

Contentment is the opposite of envy, but we can't get to the goal of contentment without recognizing what our envy is telling us about what we want, or perhaps about being able to want at all.

When we first moved to Minnesota, we had only one car, which my husband took to work each day. Our two boys were struggling to adapt to a new country, a January Minnesota winter after a January South African summer. The baby had colic and screamed a lot. One afternoon a church member picked me up and took me to her house for tea. Her older daughter took the children off to another part of the house. I sat there basking in the silence and adult conversation. Suddenly I envied this woman, her lovely, peaceful house, the time she had to herself. The envy hurt.

If I had asked myself what that envy meant, I would have realized it meant I really wanted some peace and a little time to myself. But at the time I couldn't even recognize that want. I had been taught that as a mother I could not want anything for myself, only what was best for my husband and children.

Psychologists suggest that one of the main factors behind envy is that women have often *been taught not to want.* Women often feel it is illegitimate to want or ask for things. It would not have occurred to me to ask my husband for a few hours to myself. Many women have learned that their roles are simply to make others happy, that when they feel a pang of envy they are bad and unworthy. There is usually nothing wrong with wanting and our wanting certainly needs to be looked at.

Part of Kris's problem in coming to terms with her singleness and her envy of her friends' married state is that she grew up in a home where women didn't want things. Kris's mother facilitated her husband's ministry and her children's growing up. She wouldn't have known how to say, "I don't want to move again; I want to stay here," or "I want you to be more emotionally available to me," or "I want a morning to myself." Kris's mother did not know how to really want.

Kris's envy may be more difficult for her because she finds it hard to be as passive as her mother. She finds it difficult to sit back and wait for the Lord to (maybe) bring a man. Her wanting makes her feel guilty. Envy can point to a deep conflict that women have felt about wanting.[3]

It's no good pretending we don't want things, even if we may be asked to sacrifice that desire. Let's say that at the college at which I teach, one of my colleagues publishes a book that becomes well-known in a certain discipline. Let's say she becomes known as an expert in her area of expertise and travels to a lot of conferences to speak. Back at the ranch, in the department office, people start to complain and gossip about this colleague, saying she's really not that great, complaining that she's probably neglecting her fiancé, and pointing out that all this traveling must not be very good for a person. We call this attitude "sour grapes": the ones who don't get the prize say sullenly, "Well, I wouldn't have wanted it anyhow; it wasn't much good."

Sour grapes springs from envy and may indicate several things about the colleagues who carry on so: (1) They can't admit that they are envious. Envy sounds like a bad thing and is something they seldom talk about. (2) They want what the successful colleague has got; it may tell them something about themselves, their goals and plans. (3) They disapprove of her for having wanted and gotten something.

Putting Away Envy: Admitting Our Limitations

After we've recognized our envy and seen what it is telling us about what we want and how we've felt about wanting, we need to find ways to "put away envy." Sometimes we need to recognize that our wants are not legitimate or realistic. Eve's sin in the Garden of Eden was probably one of envy. She wanted to overcome her limitedness, and that's impossible. When we get in touch with our envy we may see a desire to overcome our limitedness, to have it all. This is perhaps the most contemporary of temptations that women face. Recently women have been encouraged to believe that they could be super-women and "have it all," that they could have fulfilling careers, wonderful families, fit bodies, beautiful homes and gardens, many friends and a great intellectual life. If we have discovered the impossibility of doing everything, we may envy others who have something we don't, not realizing that they are missing something else that we have.

We need to regularly check our priorities, ask what is important and decide if we are spending our time accordingly.

The media plays a large part in promoting envy. TV shows and advertisements are able to focus our attention on certain parts of people's lives so we envy them. If you think about it, advertising is based almost exclusively on envy, suggesting that "you deserve what these people have." The media also effectively divides up people's lives. We see a person in a zippy sports car but don't hear that she lives in a two-bedroom apartment with huge unpaid bills, fights daily with her husband and suffers from infertility.

We need to repent of the attitude toward others implicit in envy. Envy is related to competition, which is central to our culture. Teachers grade on a curve, letting all members of the class know how they have done relative to one another. The results are conceit and envy. People strive to climb the corporate ladder; some move higher than others, resulting in envy and conceit. Parents strive to help their children excel in Little League, Suzuki violin, Boy Scouts, or SAT scores. Some children do better than others, and the results again are conceit and envy, for both children and parents.

The spirit of competition that is so typical of our society may be behind much of our envy and fear, according to Henri Nouwen. We believe that there is only so much to go around; if we don't get it someone else will. Envy implies limited commodities. Why should they get *x* when I don't? This spirit of competition implies a different kind of God than the one who gives so bountifully.

Envy separates us from others; we put them at an arm's length because of the strong feelings we have toward them. After coming to terms with our feelings and confessing them to God, we need to go to our sister or brother. "I'm afraid I've been distant from you since your engagement. I just couldn't handle my feelings of envy. I realize how very much I want to be married and how incomplete I feel without a man. I'm trying to work through some of that stuff, but I wanted to let you know and ask you to forgive me." We need to find perspective—God's perspective on our lives.

Putting Away Envy: Active versus Passive

We can also explore whether there are things we can do to move out of a passive state where envy (or trying not to envy) seems to be our only alternative. In other words, we can try to become active agents rather than passive victims in our life's circumstances.

For instance, when my schedule is full of teaching and writing activities and a friend tells me about her morning out with her daughter, I feel a pang of envy. I need to stop and think: "What is this telling me about what I truly want? Am I on a treadmill that I long to get off? Is it possible for me to get off?" Perhaps my envy of my friend's time with her daughter encourages me to spend more time with my own daughter.

Sometimes, as in the case of hiring a housecleaner, it is possible for me to look at my envy and see that there is something I can do about it. In other cases, like the trips to Europe, there may be nothing I can do. It would sure be nice to travel with the children. Is it possible for me to do that? Not unless I change the whole rest of my lifestyle, which I'm unwilling to do. At that point I decide to live with my twinges of envy. For me to live with those twinges keeps me from feeling like a victim to circumstances. I become an active chooser. When I hear about someone's family trip, I counter the twinge with the thought, "Yeah, it would be great. But we've made choices about the kind of family life we want, the schools we send our children to, which make a trip like that impossible for now."

Freedom from Envy

My friend Kris was wracked by her envy of people who were married. How did she respond?

First Kris recognized her envy and admitted it to herself and to her friends; it became a legitimate topic of conversation and lost some of the scary mystery that surrounded her feelings before she expressed them. Kris learned from her envy. She recognized the faulty lessons that had been drilled into her, that to want things, let alone ask for them, was selfish, demanding and not really Christian. She found a spiritual director (a wise and mature Christian woman to counsel and pray with) and met with her over a year. Kris found that she was able to be totally open with this person.

Kris's spiritual director helped her see that part of her problem was that she had grown up assuming she should take whatever life gave her, as she passively waited for it to come to her. The spiritual director suggested that Kris was all right in her "wanting" and that she needn't feel ashamed or unspiritual about it. Kris also recognized that part of her envy was based on a sense that maybe God had been unfair to her.

She also suggested that Kris should actively seek a husband.

Kris ran an advertisement in a paper for Christian singles. She was surprised after the first few dates to find that she had come to terms with her singleness much more than she thought. In dating these men, and in having a sense that she could make an active choice, she began to see her life differently. Where before she had been focusing on what seemed to be a gaping hole in her life (especially when she saw it in the light of the media that implied a woman is nothing without a man), she began to see that there was a lot she valued in her life. In fact, there were friendships and a career path that she wouldn't want to give up for marriage. She realized that although she envied her friends' marriages with their companionship and intimacy, she had perhaps been unrealistic. She wasn't sure she wanted the whole package.

Somewhere in this process Kris phoned me from California and told me she was sorry for the times she had pushed me away in her envy. She also said that she had expressed her anger toward God and repented of her lack of trust in him. Facing her envy, she learned a lot about herself. Although she may still experience twinges of envy, her envy doesn't control her life. Through recognizing her envy, listening to what it is telling her and then repenting of it and acting, she has found ways to move beyond it.

PART III

BUILDING
A HOLY LIFE

11/A QUICK FIX OR A HOLY LIFE

*O*ur society wants everything NOW! We want our mashed potatoes in three minutes, the article faxed (preferably from the car), our catalogue order express mailed, replays of football fumbles shown immediately. From our purchases to our sexual activities, our culture prefers pleasure now, payment later.[1] Magazines don't publish such articles as "A Flatter Tummy in 20 Years" or "Conquer Five Bad Habits in 35 Years."

Similarly, within the church we're not thrilled about the Nebraska farm couple's prayers, year in year out, for their errant daughter. We don't want to know about the faithful service of a pastor in a church that is *slowly* growing in size and commitment. We want to hear about churches with seven services and ten full-time staff members. Our hearty "How's it going?" becomes strained when our friend's depression goes on for months or a couple's infertility problem doesn't "clear up." TV situation comedies present crises that are solved in thirty minutes.

Quick-Fix Holiness

We know God could solve our problems (or bring us to total sanctification) in twenty-five minutes (and if he took our advice, he would). Quick fixes are popular in our society, so we want a quick-fix answer to a holy life, and we want it immediately! Often Christian speakers and writers suggest superficial, instant solutions.

At a conference in Georgia, I talked with a Christian woman who was bitter about the way she believed she had been mistreated in her life. After a vindictive tirade she said, "Well, that's just the way I am. I can't change that." Two sentences later she was telling me that she wanted people to have dramatic conversions, healings and experiences of the Holy Spirit. It's too easy to substitute the "instant gratification" of dramatic spiritual experiences for the long, hard work of dealing with past pain and bringing it to God, of cultivating the fruit of the Spirit, of building a holy life. Although the Bible gives us a realistic, long-term approach to Christian growth, often leaders within the church have tried short-cuts. One of the best quick fixes for bad behavior is fear. Fear is a very effective (if unpleasant) motivator.

Quick-Fix Good Behavior

When I was thirteen we lived in a small town in eastern Washington. Our next-door neighbors had three small children, Eddie, three; Rick, five; and Ruth, seven. For a short period I was their main babysitter.

The second time I babysat I taught the children to play "hide the button." The three-year-old, Eddie, screamed when it wasn't his turn to hide it. Ruth turned to him and said, "Eddie, remember the gun."

Eddie turned pale, his eyes opened wide. "No, no," he whimpered. Ruth said, "You be quiet or I'll get it; do you hear me?"

He started to scream hysterically. She ran to the kitchen. Eddie tore at her, "No, no don't need the gun, don't need it . . . Eddie be's good now."

Ruth moved a kitchen chair over to the cupboard above the oven. She moved a stack of *Playboy* magazines out of the way and brandished the gun, enjoying her power. I took it from her and looked at it.

"It's not real but Daddy has convinced Eddie that it is," she whispered to me conspiratorially.

I held the gun and looked down at Eddie. He clung to my legs, sobbing, "Don't shoot me, don't shoot me. I'll be good."

As a way of producing exemplary behavior in Eddie, this approach was excellent. His parents and sister could get immediate cooperation by producing (or threatening to produce) the gun. But I have often wondered what happened to Eddie. When I read about a serial murderer I half expect to see that his name is Eddie and he was born in Kennewick, Washington.

Fear is a great way to produce good short-term behavior; other deprivations also work to produce outstanding behavior in children, at least in the short term. Andrea was adopted when she was several months old; she loved her parents but had a strong sense that she needed to "perform" well in order to merit their love. When she was a child in boarding school, she often studied instead of playing because she feared that her father would lift his eyebrows in a certain way and say, "Andrea, Andrea, we're disappointed because you didn't get the best grades in the school." She needed to pay back her parents somehow for adopting her. She still feels compelled to perform to earn their love.

In child-rearing strict rules and fear tactics produce good short-term results, but through the wrong motivation we end up with the wrong long-term results—immaturity and insecurity. The church has also used fear and rules on its adherents and its enemies, threatening eternal damnation and rejection.

We don't want our children to be good just for a few years because they know who's boss and are afraid of sore backsides. We want them to learn to live responsible and holy lives motivated by love. Similarly, in our own lives we need to take a long view of holiness.

Long-Term Good Behavior

Let's say that the prodigal son's name was Dennis. You remember the story. The dad has two sons; the younger one, Dennis, is pretty rebellious as a teenager—out late, borrowing the family car and bringing it back without any gas in it, probably drinking too much. Finally he gets fed up with living at home with his dad and his know-it-all big brother so he goes into his dad's study. "Look, Dad," he says. "I know you've got plenty of money, and when you die I'll inherit some of it. Frankly, I don't want to hang around and wait. How about giving me my share now?"

Dad goes over to his wall safe, turns the knob, reaches in and takes out some bundles of bills. He counts them and says, "Here. This is your share."

Dennis yelps with joy. He grabs the money. "Can I take the old car, too?"

"Sure. I'll miss you."

Dennis belts off, chucks his stuff into the car. Dad watches from the front window as he throws it into reverse and lays some rubber heading out of the driveway.

Let's try to imagine a supper party a few weeks later. At this party are Dennis's father and Eddie's father (the one who threatens his boy with a gun). They start talking over their roast beef sandwiches.

"Say, how's Eddie?" asks Dennis's father.

"He is some kid. You have never seen a kid as obedient as he is. I say 'jump' and he says 'how high?' And I think he's going to be a whiz at math; you should see him doing multiplication tables with his sister. How's Dennis?"

"Dennis has just run away from home. He took the car and his inheritance. Rumor has it he's blowing it on prostitutes and booze in Tucson. I hope he'll be back. I love that kid."

No question about who is the most successful parent here. Eddie's dad is seeing exemplary behavior; Dennis's dad is getting some of the worst. But Dennis's behavior, dismal in the short-term, comes up trumps in the long-term, at least according to Jesus' story in the gospel. And Eddie's good behavior may be short-lived.

Why Should I Be Good?

We affirm that God is a loving heavenly father. At least at one level, we think of God as the kind of parent, like the father of the prodigal son, who stands, always watching the road, longing for his child's return.

But as we have seen, fear is a very effective way of getting people to live decent, upright lives. Good behavior, based on fear, has been promoted in a number of different strands of the Christian faith.

A Catholic friend told me that in religious education class she was told that with each fib she told to a friend, each harsh word to her sibling, she was actually driving that nail into Jesus' hand over and over again. Roman Catholic writer Gerard Hughes writes about the attitude toward God with which many Catholics grow up:

> God was a family relative, much admired by Mum and Dad, who described him as a very loving, great friend of the family, very powerful and interested in all of us. Eventually we are taken to visit "Good Old Uncle George." He lives in a formidable mansion, is bearded, gruff and threatening. We cannot share our parents' professed admiration for this jewel in the family. At the end of the visit, Uncle George turns to address us. "Now listen, dear," he begins, looking very severe, "I want to see you here once a week, and if you fail to come, let me show you what will happen to you." He then leads us down to the mansion's basement. It is dark, becomes hotter and hotter as we descend, and we begin to hear unearthly screams. In the basement there are steel doors. Uncle George opens one. "Now look in there, dear," he says. We see a nightmare vision, an array of blazing furnaces with little demons in attendance, who hurl into the blaze those men, women and children who failed to visit Uncle George or to act in a way he approved. "And if you don't visit me, dear, that is where you will most certainly go," says Uncle George. He then takes us upstairs again to meet Mum and Dad. As we go home, tightly clutching Dad with one hand and Mum with the other, Mum leans over us and says, "And now don't you love Uncle George with all your heart and soul, and mind and strength?" And we, loathing the monster, say, "Yes I do," because to say anything else would be to join the queue at the furnace. At that tender age religious schizophrenia has set in.[2]

Many Protestant attitudes are similar. In my first few years as a Christian, I lived in mortal terror of "stepping out of God's will." I heard countless testimonies about revelations, callings and (especially) couples who had met and known instantly that it was right to marry, all because the various people involved had been "at the right place at the right time." If I didn't go to Bible study tonight, or that conference that weekend, who knows? I could miss meeting Mr. Right and my life would be ruined.

What does this view—that I could step out of God's will by not making the right decision about one evening—show about my attitude toward God? My God was a distant, despotic, unpredictable father, who was willing to toss a few blessings my way as long as I was following all the rules and was attending every possible Christian meeting.

There was a bargain here: I would be loved if I was a very, very good little girl. If I wasn't a very, very good girl, my whole life would be ruined by this powerful figure. Why did I sing those choruses so enthusiastically: "I am my beloved's and he is mine, his banner over me is love"? I believe that for many Christians these cozy choruses are a desperate attempt to convince ourselves that the God we fear is good.

Good Because We're Scared?

Many of us bring an Uncle George into our Christian lives; we bring an image of a God who is despotic, authoritarian and not fully Christian. This idolatry freezes us in fear, so that we struggle to live truly holy lives. This method of keeping people "holy" is quite effective. It can lead to outwardly very good lives, at least in the short term. Inside it leads to desperate longings for acceptance and worth.

In the ministry of Jesus we see people loved and set free to belong to him. When the Son sets us free we are free indeed, says Jesus. Jesus often speaks out against fear, as Henri Nouwen points out in his book *Lifesigns.* Over and over in the Gospels we hear Jesus saying, "Do not be afraid." This reassuring voice, which repeats over and over again: "Do not be afraid, have no fear," came to Zechariah, to Mary when she was told of the impending birth of Jesus, to the women who found the stone rolled away at the tomb. "Why is there no reason to fear any longer?" Nouwen asks. Because "Jesus himself answers this question succinctly when he approaches his frightened disciples walking on the lake: 'It is I. Do not be afraid' " (Jn 6:21).[3]

We don't need to fear—not only because Jesus said it over and over but also because of the way we see Jesus interact with women in the Bible. When religious men brought a woman taken in adultery and threw her at Jesus' feet, he sent them away and spoke to her, "Neither do I condemn you. Go your way, and from now on do not sin again." When Jesus met the Samaritan woman, he did not (1) smash her, telling her to just deny herself and walk away from the sin, (2) provide a set of rules for her to follow, or (3) shame her and threaten her with a wrecked life.

What Jesus did was (1) honored her as a person by speaking to her and seeking to find out more about her life, (2) found out what her problem was and made it clear that her sin was not acceptable and (3) offered her the true water that would satisfy her desperate thirst—unconditional love.

Jesus didn't ignore this woman's sin, but he saw the need behind it and offered something that would help her build a life.

It's hard to imagine Jesus saying to the Samaritan woman, "Look, stop sleeping with this guy or your life will be more wrecked than it already is, and I'll not be your friend, and you'll never be able to do anything worthwhile in your life. Do you have kids? Oh, well, they'll be wrecked, too." Jesus treated this woman's problem as symptomatic of her far greater need for wholeness through God. He saw in her a desperate need for love and acceptance, and he filled that need.

Building a Life

When our oldest child, Andrew, was two, my husband and I read a book that encouraged a long-term approach to building a loving relationship with a child. In *How to Really Love Your Child*,[4] Ross Campbell wrote that often children's bad behavior springs out of an insecurity that asks, "Do you really love me?" Before dealing with symptoms of bad behavior, the parent must find ways to assure the child of love. Campbell suggested physical contact, eye contact and time spent alone with each child. For over eleven years now, my husband has taken Andrew out for breakfast every Saturday morning.

Building a holy life takes two things: love (which is the opposite of fear) and time. To build a holy life takes years of work, just like building the life of a child. Building a holy life is like an ongoing love relationship, in which we are intimately involved, responding to a partner. It is like family life, in which we are responsible for our part, but others help and challenge us. As in family life, we will make mistakes, fall on our faces, but others will help us up and encourage us to go on.

12/DEAD END: LEGALISM OR LICENSE

Kim is excited about her Christian life. She likes having opportunities to share her faith when she's waitressing or selling furniture. She is committed to a Bible study group; there she is beginning to take a leadership role in the study, the worship and the prayer. On Sundays she leads worship through her music ministry at church, and she often leads the congregation in prayer. But Kim's most striking quality is difficult to describe. She seems to be "free"—happy with who she is, content with her small apartment and her jobs, satisfied to be growing as a Christian within a community of people who care about her. Kim is confident, funny, intelligent and holy. She reminds me of the story that Matthew tells about the woman who came to Jesus with an alabaster jar; she breaks it to show her love for Jesus (Mt 26:7-13). There is joy when we give ourselves fully to Jesus. That's fixing our hearts where true joy is to be found.

Kim has not always been like this; in fact she arrived at this freedom when she was nearly thirty-five. In the years before, she had tried the ever-popular freedom substitutes: legalism and license. Kim has now found freedom through responsible belonging in a Christian community. (We'll look at that in the next chapter.)

Legalism and license are two dead ends on the journey to holiness and freedom. Jesus is our model of Christian freedom. He can set his people free from rules and free from sin.

Legalism: Can't Live with It

If we treat legalism as an answer to child-rearing problems, this is what we hear: "Put enough rules, and good strict rules, in place, and the kids will know where they stand. Then they'll behave themselves." But Jesus shunned this approach.

Jesus was born into a rule-keeping culture, yet he treated sinners with great tenderness. It was the Pharisees, the legalists who offered another "quick-fix" answer to sin and temptation, with whom Jesus was most impatient. He called them whited sepulchers, blind guides. They were the ones who were proud and self-righteous; they imposed long sets of rules on people. Jesus reserved any "smashing" for the Pharisees.

Kim grew up in a legalistic family. Her father was an elder in the church, but he often told jokes against other races and women. Kim was impressed with the ministers in these churches: "They had carefully groomed hair and wore proper, nerdy suits. They looked nervous about their appearance, adjusting their ties, pulling at their vests, checking that their shoes were polished and their socks pulled up. I remember watching them and wondering why they cared so much about how they looked."

Kim found church boring, but she knew she should like it. One of her earliest memories was of being at the church for a wedding reception. "My brother and I slipped upstairs to the sanctuary and pretended to be the pastor. I had to climb onto a box, and then I stood there, thumping my fist on the edge of the pulpit and shouting, shouting. That's what pastors did. They made people feel bad."

At home Kim learned that the main virtue was "niceness." The opposite of "niceness" was getting angry or saying what you really felt. That was called being "ugly" and was something that Jesus didn't like. There were countless things that Jesus didn't like. One Sunday school song used to scare her:

Be careful little mouth what you say,

Be careful little mouth what you say,

For the Father up above is looking down in love,

Be careful little mouth what you say.

Then all the other verses continued, "Be careful little hands what you touch; Be careful little eyes what you see. . . ." Kim felt that she had to be good to be loved; she had to repress her emotions and always be nice and reasonable.

When Kim was a young high school student her parents started to fight a lot. It turned out that her father was having an affair. Kim sat outside their bedroom door at night listening to them fight, and then on Sunday they all went to church together. Eventually Kim stopped going to church because it seemed meaningless, but it didn't affect her belief in God. For Kim there were two totally different parts of religion: the real God and human, rule-breaking parents.

Kim saw the emptiness of legalism. But legalism is not only

emptiness, it also soaks up a tremendous amount of energy. Legalism is the opposite of holiness because it diverts attention from the vital to the trivial. At some colleges that have "lifestyle statements" more time seems to be spent discussing the lifestyle statement than how to serve Jesus, love one another, or think through political and ethical issues. Absolute "thou shalt nots" draw extraordinary focus and energy, which may explain why Jesus avoided them and was called a "wine-bibber and a glutton." Jesus was consistently criticized for being the friend of tax-collectors and sinners, and this was how he replied:

"Now, you Pharisees clean the outside of the cup and of the dish, but inside you are full of greed and wickedness. . . . Woe also to you lawyers! For you load people with burdens hard to bear, and you yourselves do not lift a finger to ease them" (Lk 11:39-52).

Legalism promotes self-righteousness and emphasis on externals, which we have equated with pride. Legalism is like saying, "I will know that I've been a successful parent to my daughter if she is always in by 10:30 and not a minute later." Legalism encourages immaturity, obsessive thinking and ultimately rebellion. Nouwen expresses it like this: "While Jesus showed a high regard for the observance of the Jewish law, he attacked fear-and-power-motivated legalism and clearly demonstrated that the law should always be in the service of the divine work of love."[1] Paul encourages Christians to be circumcised in their hearts, not their bodies (Rom 2:29).

Legalism is a security blanket, which is attractive to us, because it makes us feel as if everything is settled and safe. A set of rules seems so simple; we follow the code and we're fine. Legalism also protects us from anything mysterious and outside our experience.[2] Interestingly enough, legalism seems to be most prevalent when the biblical teaching on a subject is unclear. The Scriptures often offer principles rather than rules. A principle such as "our bodies are temples of the Holy Spirit" has to be applied with wisdom. We'd prefer a simple rule.

At a housegroup meeting the other night, a couple spoke. "If we look tired," she said, "it is because we've been staying up until two or three every morning talking. We're trying to work through the legalism that was laid on us for so many years. We're realizing how it has warped our views of God and even of Jesus. I realize that to me Jesus was actually a Pharisee. I mean, I grew up believing that if he was a good man, he must have been a rule-keeper."

"Yes," the husband said, "and if we weren't involved in a community of faith who love God and want to serve him, we might have just burned out of Christianity altogether."

Another group member agreed. "It took me months of coming to the Church of the Messiah to get over legalism. Each Sunday morning I'd wake up to my old Sunday morning blues, and I'd think, Oh, no, it's Sunday and I have to go to church or else I'll be in trouble. Then my adult tape would switch on and run through my mind, Yeah, but you're grown up; you live on your own now, you don't have to go anywhere. I gradually realized that I *wanted* to be in church. I'd get there and think, Hey, this is where I want to be! I like to be at church and in God's presence. But it took me months before that filtered through and began to dominate my first thoughts on Sunday mornings. There'd been so many years of *oughts.*"

Legalism as a Path to Rebellion

Legalism doesn't work, at least in the long term. If I submit myself to the legalism of a diet, the effect is usually to make me unable to think about anything but food. Legalism can promote obsessive behavior; I find myself doing things I don't even really want to do because I have been commanded not to do them.

Legalism promotes the "forbidden fruit" syndrome. Small excesses or pleasures assume massive proportions so that watching an R-rated movie or dancing becomes vastly appealing. And this leads to the worst outcome of legalism—rebellion. Most thinking people cannot remain constrained by legalism because it so clearly runs counter to the teaching of Jesus and Paul in the New Testament. The break that they make with legalism may spell disaster.

Kim rebelled against the legalism of her childhood. She recognized the superficiality of her parents' legalism. Kim's sister Becky had acted out her pain over their parents' divorce by finding a man who would look after her and tell her what to do. Becky belonged to a church like the one their parents had taken her to. She started pushing Kim to lose weight and find a man. She explained to Kim that her own husband would not have married her if she hadn't lost weight; he had told her that. So if Kim wanted a man she would have to lose weight.

For Kim the burden of childhood legalism and shame crashed in on her. Her low self-esteem and her doubts about her body seemed overwhelming. Kim decided she needed to prove that she could be attractive to someone. When she looked at her Christian faith it looked like a bunch of petty rules, so she figured the rule against fornication was just another. Kim started thinking it was pretty dumb to be thirty years old and still a virgin. "One of the guys at work, I'd told him I was, and he walked around for a week saying, 'Humm, thirty-year-old virgin; really rare.' " Kim wondered if her sister was right; maybe she would never marry. "What if I never get married? Never have sex? Forget that!" Kim threw off her legalism.

Kim found someone who treated her just as her father had.

Cal was older; he had money and bought her things. Like her father, he didn't listen to her; she had to figure out when Cal was in just the right mood so she could talk to him. Otherwise he would lose his temper. They got along because Kim was willing to compromise. "He treated me just like my father had and I loved it and hated it." Kim knew right from the beginning where the relationship was headed.

For six weeks Cal and Kim slept together. "I knew he was a jerk. I didn't like him at all, and yet there I was sleeping with him. Part of me thought he'd change; I've got a good imagination and for me sex had always seemed special, so I guess I couldn't allow myself to believe that this relationship was as awful as it was."

Then one Saturday afternoon, she suddenly wanted to know that he cared about her. "I wasn't asking him to pledge his undying love or marry me or anything. He could have just told me I was cute or fun. I asked him, 'So hey, what do you think of me?' "

"You're bothering me. Just leave me alone."

"I'm not going to until you tell me what you think of me." He ignored her and walked into the other room.

She followed him and asked him again. "Will you damn well leave me alone?" he shouted.

"I should have walked out then, but my mother had taught me always to be nice. I waited awhile and apologized to him, and then made up a lame excuse about needing to feed some cats. Then I left. He wouldn't even tell me that he liked me." Kim feels that she lost something, something irretrievable, and that she wasted it on a creep.

Kim rebelled, and that is not unusual. Unlike the freedom and abundant life that Jesus promises, legalism constricts and chokes. License is the answer that many people give to legalism.

Legalism provides a lifestyle that most people should grow out of, but legalism does not throw off its shackles in a reasonable way. Legalism ends up throwing its former adherents toward sin. It "leads them into temptation."

License: A Poor Substitute

License is terrible, but often it is a cry of pain, a response to the shaming of heavy-handed theology or the immaturity of legalism. If people cannot live with legalism and don't belong to a helping community of faith, then it is little wonder that they follow the world's maxims: "feel free" or "do it if it feels good."

License is as damaging as legalism. It fails to take adequate account of either human sinfulness or the strength of society's lies. Our society tells us that anything goes, that we should feel free to do our own thing. License is a poor substitute for true freedom. Even if we are no longer listening to a church, college or parental authority, in license we are allowing the world to tell us what is important.

Jean and Mandy are talking. Jean is an active Christian who still struggles with a legalistic upbringing. Mandy has only been a Christian for just over a year, since shortly after her second divorce. She has two young sons and has struggled financially and socially. Recently she started dating a doctor who isn't a Christian.

Jean: "So, how's it going with Len, Mandy?"

Mandy: "I really like him, and it's so neat to eat out and go to concerts without counting every penny. But he's not a believer at all. Says he's not interested in God. I don't know what I should do about that."

Jean: "Well, he's a great guy and at your age you can't wait forever. I'd go for it if I were you."

The world tells Jean and Mandy that a woman is nothing

without a man. The church has underlined that. The Scriptures teach that a person should not become deeply involved with someone whose spiritual center is so different. License invites the Christian to listen to the "wisdom" of the world, and says, "Feel free."

" 'All things are lawful,' but not all things are beneficial," Paul wrote in 1 Corinthians 10:23. We as women have been too prone to listen to any voice that will tell us what to do because of our poor self-image; we have found it very hard to stand up and say no. And many voices will be telling us to have fun.

Jesus says that "everyone who commits sin is a slave to sin" (Jn 8:34). Most of us know this slavery: lured by temptation, caught by sin and imprisoned by a downward spiral of guilt. Legalism is a dead end and so is license. Neither one is freedom. Kim found freedom in a community of faith as she learned to be real with herself, with others, and with God. God intends this freedom for all of his people.

13/BEING REAL WITH OURSELVES, OTHERS & GOD

Michelle ran away. *She was fifteen and was tired of the restrictions* of a family that told her what to do. She was weary of curfews and dress codes. She ran off to find people who would really appreciate her.

I asked Michelle's father what they'd heard. "Well, the people she ran off with dumped her when they found out she was a runaway, because they don't want the police on them. Got a call today from a guy who was with her . . . he didn't like the way a group she was hanging out with was treating her, so he phoned the police. I guess my prayer is that she will hit a low enough point that she begins to see things clearly."

The prodigal son "came to himself." He recognized that he had been silly to run away from home, that he'd been wasting himself, that he had been hurting others. He recognized his sin. He knew he could go home, that he could meet his father again and that his father would forgive. Until Michelle "comes to herself"—begins to be real with herself and others—she cannot grow.

Hypocrisy happens when people don't "come to themselves," when they allow themselves and each other not to be real. Ananias and Sapphira wanted to look holy and committed without being that (Acts 5:1-11). It didn't work.

The downfalls of a number of celebrity Christians a few years ago revealed people whose positions had not allowed them to be real with themselves and others. They had surrounded themselves with people who idolized them. When this happens, it is effortless for a person to think, "I'm awfully important; the rules don't apply to me. I don't really mean to do wrong. I won't tell anyone. Just think how it would upset people to know the real me." Lack of recognizing our weaknesses, lack of being real with self, others and God leads to disaster.

Recognizing our sin is the prerequisite to belonging to a community of faith. Recognizing our sin is being real with ourselves, others and God about our humanity—and it is a prerequisite to forgiveness, freedom and growth.

Being Real with Ourselves

We need to see our failings clearly and name them to ourselves. Seeing our sin can be difficult. If our sin was not entirely our fault, it can be especially hard to name it as sin.

Ginni's family was dysfunctional. Her father was an alcoholic and her mother enabled his behavior. Ginni lacked confidence and found her only satisfaction and sense of worth in helping others. When she finished a degree in chemistry, she met a man named Brad. Brad was fun to be around, but under the surface he needed someone to look after him. It seemed to Ginni that he was all that she wasn't, and he needed her. He asked her to move in with him, and she did.

Two years later Ginni started medical school. Brad moved with her to North Carolina. When she finished medical school and started her residency, things came to a crisis. "I began to get lots of praise for my medical work," she said. "I began to realize that maybe I was a worthwhile person in my own right. I looked at Brad and realized that I had connected with him because I needed someone who needed me and someone who in some way would protect me and care for me. Here I was, twenty-seven years old and basically still reacting to my childhood wounds. I had lived with Brad for seven years, without really liking him, without his being the kind of person I could imagine marrying or having children with. I wasn't sure that I had ever liked him."

After her first residency, Ginni decided to move to another area to do further research work. She broke up with Brad. Although she knew she had to, it was very hard for her to do. For the first time in years, she and Brad lived apart.

In her new job, Ginni met Christians and became one. She also met another man named Vince. They dated and fell in love, but their relationship seemed to be stuck. It was stuck on Brad. Vince felt that Brad's presence haunted their relationship. Ginni felt that although her relationship with Brad hadn't been great, she had learned a lot from those eight years. After two years, Vince and Ginni broke up. Ginni did a lot of thinking.

A few months later Vince and Ginni met again and shortly afterwards got engaged. "We weren't able to take our relationship further until I could come to a point where I recognized that my long relationship with Brad was an unhealthy thing. It had been a sick reaction to a sick family life, and it had been a waste of all those years.

"It may seem odd that it was hard for me to see that, but to say that was to say that I was responsible for all those years not being all they could be. That felt overwhelming to me. But until I did, Vince and I could not properly grieve those years, and I couldn't ask God's forgiveness, and we couldn't move on. We were stuck."

Ginni had to be real with herself; this led to her being real with others and with God.

Being Real with Others
Temptation is a great leveler. All of us face temptation, and it can often drive us to our knees. If our friend's sin seems more dramatic than ours, we need to think, "There but for the grace of God go I." It is tempting to point fingers at other's sins. We may condemn someone else's adultery but forget our own pride and greed.

Unconfessed sin becomes more destructive with time, like the monster created by Victor Frankenstein. If we cannot share our sins or our temptations with someone, they begin to loom out of all proportion. Our culture encourages isolation and individualism, and the church has often followed the culture. We guard our family's privacy. We can be superficial even in small groups in the church. When we isolate ourselves, either by not spending time with others or by being superficial, we lose a God-given resource for holiness.

When I had been a Christian several years, I lived in a house with a few other women. My roommate and I were close; her name was Mary Lou. She and I talked until all hours of the night.

At the time I was struggling with overeating. I would often stop in at Baskin-Robbins whether I was hungry or not, buy a nice big ice cream sundae and wolf it down. Afterwards I felt terrible. I pulled out Bible verses that seemed to fit with my problem and memorized them on long, painful runs, verses like, "Do you not know that your body is a temple of the Holy Spirit within you?"

One evening as Mary Lou and I talked, I hinted at some terrible sin that was haunting me. She asked if I would like to tell her about it. I tried but couldn't. I felt so condemned, so wicked about this overeating.

For several evenings Mary Lou tried to elicit my confidence. Finally on about the fourth night, I managed to push myself into telling her about my secret sin.

There was a long silence in the dark. Finally she said, "Is that all? I thought at least you were having an affair with some professor or something." Silence and isolation breed a lack of proportion.

We need others to whom we can confess our sins. Once I had admitted my overeating to a friend, she could help me in four ways: (1) She could correct my skewed perspective. Not talk me out of it ("Everybody does it; I'm sure it doesn't bother God; it's not really *sin*"), but help me see that I wasn't the total unforgivable slob I felt like. (2) We could pray together; I could receive God's forgiveness and make a fresh start. (3) We could figure out what this problem said about my lack of self-worth, about my need to please and perhaps even about my attitude toward God. (4) We could establish some sort of accountability so she could help me deal with the daily challenge.

Kathy had always felt her temptations were much worse than those of other women she knew. She felt she had a major problem with lust, one which other women never seemed to face. She began to feel that it was so serious that even God would not be able to forgive her.

A counselor listened to Kathy and said, "Hey, welcome to the human race."

Kathy realized that she wasn't outrageous; she was tempted exactly as many others are. She suddenly felt able to go to God and ask for grace. Kathy's temptation had regained proportion as she confessed to another person. There is something very healing about confessing to another person. I wonder if, in the Protestant tradition, with our emphasis on going straight to God, we haven't lost something wonderful in losing the practice of confession.

Henri Nouwen concludes, "Much suffering is caused by the fear of confessing and asking forgiveness. I have seen the most radical changes in the lives of people when they finally found the courage to confess what they felt most ashamed of or most guilty about and discovered that instead of losing a friend they gained one. Distances were bridged, walls came tumbling down, and abysses were filled in."[1]

Forgiveness by others leads to a sense of being accepted by God.

Being Ourselves with God

"The thing that really gets me," my friend tells me, "is the way you come to terms with a temptation; you feel like, 'well that's one I won't have to deal with again,' and you relax and put your feet up and it whacks you from behind. Just like that. You look at it and sure enough . . . same temptation that you just finished dealing with once and for all."

We need each other desperately because we are subject to paralyzing condemnation. When added to the low self-esteem many women experience, the condemnation we hear from the evil one can lead us into a downward spiral of greater and greater self-loathing. We need to learn to differentiate between the conviction of the Spirit and the condemnation of the evil one.

"Clearly the Enemy seeks to destroy your fellowship with God," writes John White. "The Spirit, on the other hand, is attempting to restore your fellowship with God. . . . Now if the Spirit is attempting to restore your fellowship with God, it follows that when sin is confessed, conviction will melt away and the blossom of fellowship burst out with a new fragrance. It also follows that if Satan is bent on destroying your fellowship with God and if your sense of sin results from satanic accusation, then no such fragrance will be experienced."

When we confess to God, we need to be clear what we are confessing and then claim God's forgiveness for it. If we begin to feel bad again, we can then remember the promises of God. Sometimes, it's helpful to use a written prayer, so that we don't pray "vague thoughts" and later wonder whether we actually prayed or not. (For some specific prayers of confession, see the appendix.)

A tree expert looked at the trees in our garden. When he came to the apple tree he said, "This needs a good pruning."

"I find it really hard to cut bits out of a tree," I said. "It seems so cruel and final to hack away at a living thing."

"See this branch," he said. "No apples on it, and it just takes energy from the tree. If it's not here, then the tree has a chance to grow better."

That's what our sin is like, I thought. It's like extra branches that soak up the energy. But in order to get rid of those extra branches, we need help. An apple tree may shed branches in a windstorm, but usually it cannot prune itself. We need to confess—to the Lord who forgives, and also sometimes to other people. Then we will find in a community of faith the pruning help we need.

Responsible Belonging

Responsible belonging is the answer to building Christian holiness. This process of learning to be *real* is what will enable us to belong responsibly in a community of faith.

Manny, Greta and Mike are recent graduates of a Christian college, all from similar, legalistic backgrounds where they had been told (or at least feel that they were told) how to think and behave. They started attending our church and coming to the housegroup that I lead.

One Sunday none of them were in church. At the housegroup meeting that Tuesday, Manny said, "Well, the party at our house Saturday night was so great! It went until three o'clock, but it was sure worth it."

Greta added, "Great party! Slept till noon on Sunday. I thought the church police would be over, but they weren't."

Mike spoke: "Well, yes, it was a great party. What was weird was that I actually kind of missed church on Sunday."

"Irresponsible kids!" I was thinking, feeling pretty annoyed at them by this time. Then I realized that like children, they were testing the boundaries. They were learning to be in church because they were a part of it, they *belonged,* rather than because there were some rules that forced them or a parent who told them off for "bad" behavior. They would learn that part of belonging was commitment and responsibility, the kind of dependability that makes trust and deep relationships possible. They would learn to deepen their roots with others in this community; they would learn to share the loads of the Christian community as mature, responsible Christians.

14/RESPONSIBLE BELONGING IN A COMMUNITY OF FAITH

*T*eresa *was a manager in a restaurant. She enjoyed the customers,* the tips and the responsibility, but her boss was becoming more and more abusive. He pinched her and slapped her bottom behind the counter. When she threatened to quit he pleaded with her to stay, telling her that the restaurant would suffer without her. One evening after Bible study group, Teresa wept as she told us how much she despised her boss but how helpless she felt because of the way he manipulated her and because she depended on her salary and tips.

June, Amanda and I told Teresa that she needed to quit, that she was worth more than this kind of abuse. Teresa cried some more and agreed that she would quit the next morning. We agreed to meet her to celebrate her courageous move. We waited and waited for her, and at 8:30 we went to the restaurant. We walked in and sat in a booth. She brought us water. "Hi. I decided I'd better finish out the month. He wants me to."

"Teresa, this situation is bad for you. You agreed about that last night."

"Do you think I should quit now?" She looked at all our faces and we nodded.

"You're right. I know you're right. I'll grab my stuff and tell him and meet you out in the car." As we walked out Teresa's boss glowered at us. We heard later that he ranted for days about those "leddies from the church."

Teresa belonged to a church family that cared about her and was available to help her do what she knew she needed to do. It is as we are responsible members of a community of faith that we are able to grow in our individual lives of faith.

Every time we pray the Lord's prayer, we pray, "Lead us not into temptation." How can we cooperate with God, so that we are not led into temptation?

"Okay," you might say. "I can see how I've been led into temptation before. I've tried answers to my temptations that haven't worked. I tried the ever popular breaking-the-spirit, smashing-the-self approach, and that sure didn't work. I know that a set of rules is counterproductive. I also realize that many people's reaction to legalism—a feel-free approach—is a way of bolting headlong into sin. I can see that one way of not being led into temptation is to be real with myself, others and God. What else?"

What do we do if we want to help a child in our family with a problem? We find ways of making sure that the child knows she is loved and senses she is a full member of the family. We encourage her to take her place as a responsible member who knows she belongs.

Christians are part of a body, a community, in which they function as they are meant to. It is here that they will learn to value themselves, to recognize their feelings, to see what they are substituting for God. It is here that they will begin to find the right balance of belonging and responsibility. It is here that they will explore with others the implications of Holy Scripture on their lives, that they will pray and discover the power of the Holy Spirit to transform their lives. Perhaps most important, it is within the community that they will find an active and fulfilling ministry. As they grow in their responsible belonging in a community of faith, they cooperate with God by not being led into temptation but instead building a holy and joy-filled life.

Lead Me Not into Temptation: Lead Me Away from Self-Doubt
Only as we learn to value ourselves can we begin to be fully invested in other relationships. What does it mean to feel better about ourself? It means authenticity, being the same person in different relationships, despite their different demands.

We have progressed further on the scale of valuing ourselves when we are able to do the following:

☐ present a balanced picture of both our strengths and our vulnerabilities;

☐ make clear statements of our beliefs, values and priorities, and then keep our behavior congruent with these;

☐ stay emotionally connected to significant others when things get pretty intense;

☐ address difficult and painful issues and take a position on matters important to us;

☐ state our differences and allow others to do the same.[1]

In the community of faith, a woman will find that she is loved and supported for more important qualities than her good looks or her ability to cook. As we have seen, the woman who doubts her own worth and feels unloved is much more vulnerable to sin.

Lead Me Not into Temptation: Lead Me into Greater Self-Recognition
We have seen that women who do not understand their emotions may be much more vulnerable to sin than those who do. My psychologist friend talks about how challenging it is to help women find out who they are, especially when previously they have only found themselves within someone else's life. In the community of faith, as people come to know us as we are, they will help us see our weaknesses and our strengths. We will learn to "confess [our] sins to one another, and pray for one another, so that [we] may be healed" (Jas 5:16).

Angie had allowed herself to become emotionally involved with a married neighbor. She felt ashamed and didn't tell any of her friends until one night after Bible study. As the Bible study leader talked with her, Angie said, "But I've never had a man who seemed to really find me so attractive. It means a lot to me." Angie's community members were able to point out to her that she was worth more than this, that she had thought of herself in such lowly terms that she was taking whatever crumbs she could get from this man. They helped her see that she deserved better. And they helped her see that she was deeply loved by God.

Lead Me Not into Temptation: Lead Me Away from Substitutes
In the community of faith, as we get to know each other well and as accountability grows, we will be able to encourage each other not to trust the wrong things, not to rely on externals.

Often in our own lives, it's hard to find perspective; this is something that we can help each other do.

When I was expecting our second child, my husband was offered the opportunity to visit some churches in the United States. He was excited about bringing some ideas from these churches back into our parish in Cape Town. I was devastated. Six weeks without my husband! One day I had tea with an older woman in the church. "How are you?" she asked.

I sighed. "I find it so awful when Ernie's not around. I feel only half here, and so I just kind of wander around."

"It kinda makes you wonder who your first love is, doesn't it?" she asked.

I was speechless. I felt angry. But I respected her as a woman and a friend. That night I thought about what she had said to me and asked God to forgive me for substituting my husband for God. Since then I miss Ernie when we are apart, but some of the desperation is gone.

Lead Me Not into Temptation: Lead Me Away from Individualism

"Most Americans see religion as something individual, prior to any organizational involvement"; in fact a Gallup poll conducted in 1978 found that eighty percent of Americans agree that "an individual should arrive at his or her own religious beliefs independent of any churches or synagogues."[2] We promote a personal walk with God, inviting a person to "accept Jesus Christ as her personal Lord and Savior." We promote individual confession (only myself and God), personal quiet times and tiny individual communion cups. All of these emphasize the individual believer's relationship with God. But this is only part of the picture, one side of the coin. An individual's relationship to other Christians is almost as important. Her relationship to

God will be facilitated through other Christians; many times others will "be Christ" to her or she to them.

If we can't manage quite easily on our own, we feel something is wrong, but as Christians we are not *meant* to manage on our own. The Christianity of the New Testament teaches that Christians belong to one another, are members one of another and are members of a body together.

Lead Me Not into Temptation: Lead Me Away from Unhealthy Dependency

We need community to live a Christian life. As women we are fortunate because we were raised to value our relationships with others. This is wonderful, but we need to guard against a dependency that lets us be irresponsible or allows us to be dishonest with ourselves.

"Our upbringing as girls prepares us to be receptive, giving, thoughtful, kind, solicitous; to take account of one another, to see things from the other person's point of view; to feel ourselves in another person's shoes. But these are not simple lessons we learn like algebraic formulas or our times tables; they are rather the grammar of women's emotional experience, the internal declension that organizes our relationships to others and self."[3]

Our upbringing, our tendency to value relationships can be a wonderful gift but can also lead to unhealthy and compulsive concerns for others. Sometimes we slip into attachments in which we lose ourselves in each other's needs.[4] When a woman has known and defined herself in terms of her relationships, she may have mixed feelings about having time for herself. She may have had no experience of being involved in relationships as a healthy individual; she has so frantically cared for others that she has carefully avoided caring for herself.[5] What seems to be difficult for a woman is finding the fine balance where she is truly invested in relationships and yet able to be herself, where she takes responsibility for herself as well as for others. This was Martha's conflict—so busy taking care of everybody that she was unable to take time with Jesus as Mary was doing.

When I first considered going back to college to finish my degree, I knew that the idea was preposterous. I had "found myself" in my family, my husband. How could I, a woman who had done nothing but cook and clean and look after children, presume to go to college? I'll never forget the day that changed.

When I saw two young women with their black graduation gowns flapping in the May breeze, something entirely unexpected happened in my head. I had been patiently assuring Susannah that we would be home soon and then I would give her a nice cookie, but her cries faded from my mind as if someone had pressed the mute button on the remote control. *I have to return to college.* Ten seconds before, I was the total mother, absolutely responsive to my children, patiently driving them to zoo classes and music lessons. Ten seconds earlier it would have seemed impossible that my diapered, sleep-disturbed brain could ever be capable of a paper or a test. The decision to go back to college was instantaneous, as if God had reached down out of the sky, placed a cosmic frame around those two St. Catherine's students and said to me, "You will finish your college degree."

Maybe I shouldn't do it. Instantly there were doubts. Wouldn't my children miss me if I took a class, and what would people in the church think if their minister's wife went to college? There was also a part of me that knew I couldn't do it. Ask me about anything more philosophical than breastfeeding or sidewalk coloring and I couldn't answer.

Women who have "found themselves" in certain relationships feel secure there. Coupled with low self-esteem, this leads women to stay within safe roles rather than to step out and try something new. I was fortunate to have a husband and church friends who were wonderfully supportive. But there are many situations where women spiral into worse and worse self-doubt.

Responsible belonging in the community is not about women being totally wrapped up in the lives of others at the expense of their own lives. It is about intimacy in the best sense of that word.

"Intimacy is not a happy medium. It is a way of being in which the tension between distance and closeness is dissolved and a new horizon appears. Intimacy is beyond fear. Those who have experienced the intimacy to which Jesus invites us know that they no longer need to worry about getting too close or becoming too distant. When Jesus says, 'Do not be afraid; it is I,' he reveals a new space in which we can move without fear. This intimate space is not a fine line between distance and closeness, but a wide field of movement in which the question of whether we are close or distant is no longer the guiding question."[6]

The closeness of community is a closeness in which *we set each other free to live for Jesus,* a closeness in which we challenge each other to grow by trying some new form of ministry, a new profession, or a new relationship.

Eva had become a lawyer in the days when there were few women lawyers. There was a lot of status in being a lawyer. Although she got a good, prestigious job, she hated it. In her Bible study group, she talked about her work and how it didn't satisfy her. The group encouraged her to look into other kinds of work, to get career counseling. She discovered that she liked working with children. Eva courageously left her law firm and returned to school to get her teaching credentials. With the support of a community she was able to see what she really wanted and move in a new direction.

In the Community: Lead Me into the Scriptures and a Christian Mind

Within the Christian community we need to study the Scriptures together. Biblical teaching and preaching can be very helpful for giving us a foundation of Christian truth, but they are not enough. Sermons and Sunday School lessons give us biblical truth, but only from one person's perspective, and biblical truth cannot be captured by one person. We need to be involved with others in Bible study, investing time in digging into and meditating on the Scriptures for ourselves.

In order to build a holy life, we need an overall understanding of God's perspective. Throughout the ages, good, well-meaning Christians have supported dreadful oppression by pulling prooftexts from the Scriptures. They have taught that slavery was fine, war was admirable, women should be treated like children, Sabbath-breakers deserved dreadful punishments.

To gain an overall understanding of Scripture, we need to study with others and to read the Bible in chunks. We need to read books written by Christians and about Christians' lives. We need to develop a perspective on issues through hearing speakers, reading and discussing with other Christians. We need to puzzle over the verses that bother us and wonder why they make us uncomfortable.

When I first became a Christian I went to lots of Bible studies. A Bible teacher taught us; he had found verses that supported his particular perspective on the Bible and he served those up to us. My sense was that each verse was true in itself, a promise to claim. But we avoided certain verses.

I started reading Luke. In chapter four I got my first shock. Here's Jesus in the synagogue at Nazareth, and what does he choose to read? About how people would know the Messiah had come by good news being preached to the poor, release to the captives, sight to the blind and liberty to the oppressed (Lk 4:18). How could Jesus, I wondered, have been so "social gospel"? Why couldn't he have launched his ministry with an Old Testament passage that fit better with the theology I was learning at Bible study?

A day or two later, I came across the passage in Matthew 25 where Jesus tells about how the sheep will be separated from the goats. I was stunned to find that Jesus seemed to take feeding the hungry, clothing the naked and visiting prisoners so seriously. Didn't Jesus, of all people, know that the just are saved by faith?

I closed my Bible. It took me some time to realize that if I was uncomfortable with a passage in the Bible I needed to look at it and see what it was saying to me, perhaps about a blind spot I had.

We need life in the community so that we can challenge each other. As individuals we have certain passages we like to skip. As a group we can discuss what it means that we should "hate our fathers and mothers and children" and whether Jesus was suggesting a new priority of relationships. We can wonder together about what Jesus meant when he said that we should sell everything (Mt 19:21). The gospel is radical; together we must learn to work that out in our lives.

Lead Me into Prayer and the Power of the Spirit
Within a community of faith we will find the power to be disciples. This may come in many different forms. We may pray for Phyllis that she will find peace as she is guided by God. For

Susan (who has emotional wounds from childhood and a very poor self-image that make her susceptible to a certain temptation) we ask that some of those deep wounds and memories will be healed. We may listen to and pray with Connie for forgiveness from a past sin that has dogged her.

I picked up the phone one evening and a voice sobbed on the other end, "Mary Ellen, I'm spotting. I'm afraid I'm having a miscarriage and Phil is out of town."

"I'll be right over."

Dory had a miscarriage. But worse than the miscarriage was her guilt. The miscarriage was her fault, she told me, because she had had an abortion when she was only sixteen. That was twelve years before, and she was living with the guilt; she knew God hadn't forgiven her, so how could she forgive herself?

Dory needed a member of the community of faith to be with her physically and emotionally. She needed someone to confess to, someone to pray with, someone to help her find God's forgiveness for a sin committed before she had become a Christian. She needed God's help in building on this foundation.

Our church has a healing ministry that goes on Sunday by Sunday during communion. I go up for prayer, not only if my neck is sore, but also if I'm feeling fearful, or if I want prayer about certain temptations that I'm experiencing. I could pray about these matters myself, but it is within the body of Christ that I expect to find healing. I also find accountability as a friend like Jim says to me, "Well how's it going with those fears?"

Lead Me into Active Ministry

Imagine Mother Teresa berating herself for hours about eating an extra chocolate-chip cookie. When we as women become involved in active ministry, we find healthier ways of looking at our lives. Holiness becomes not only a wonderful end in itself, but a means to an end, a powerful vehicle for service. We must find ways of using our gifts for God.

This is why women should no longer be asked to deny their ministries for the sake of men's ministries. An active ministry leads to holiness; it also leads to more work being accomplished for the kingdom of God. Shifting women into active, challenging ministry may mean a certain amount of inconvenience; men may need to learn how to work the coffee makers or organize potlucks.

Several years ago *Christianity Today* had a page of obituaries for some great Christian men who had died within a short period of time. These men had done impressive work for God. They had founded missionary societies, magazines, colleges; they had written books and articles and taught young Christians. But I couldn't help but wonder how much more work might have been accomplished for God if an equal number of women had been encouraged in their ministries. On the Judgment Day I wouldn't want to be in the shoes of men who have squelched women's ministries, trying to explain why I had discouraged the talents and ministries of more than half of the Christian community.

When we share Christ with a needy person, our lives slide into perspective, a perspective that counteracts the world's messages to us in the media. We begin to see what is really important, rather than what we are told is important. Temptations that would like to hold center stage in our lives are forced offstage as we involve ourselves in active ministry and others' lives.

We find in active ministry real joy as we use our talents to do the work of the kingdom. And this in turn leads to a healthy perspective and true holiness of life.

Epilogue

At the beginning of this book we heard the story of Jill's fall into adultery. How was she able to turn her life around?

"I am just grateful to God that I found a church that has been an oasis to me and people who were willing to accept me, set me on my feet and encourage me in my journey with Jesus. I very nearly threw it all out, I felt so shamed." Jill has found healing through responsible belonging to a community of faith.

"I don't think I could admit how shriveled-up my own heart was from the pain—the shame and guilt I felt for a lifetime of looking to others for approval and security and for divorcing Gavin and hurting so many people, especially my children and our families." Within a church family, Jill has found a place where she is known, recognized and accepted.

"It was in this group of people that I began to be *real* with myself, others and with God. I felt totally accepted, warts and all, and at the same time challenged by them to restructure many areas of my life." She has asked members of her small Bible study group to help in her vulnerable areas. "I've made myself accountable to friends in the church. I've told them to check on me and I have pledged myself to tell them if I'm feeling weak or tempted." She knows that if she is feeling anxious she is apt to resort to relying on her looks. "When I was offered a choice of consulting regions in either Michigan or Los Angeles, I chose Michigan because I felt that I might be less prone there to play on my sexuality, my attractiveness." Within the community Jill has an active ministry, where she is involved in pastoral care, and prays for those who need healing. She finds that being able to help others is as exciting as childbirth. "I don't ever want to forget how thrilling it is to be available to God and to be used by him." She believes that it is impossible to live the Christian life apart from a community of Christians to support and challenge and give her perspective on her life.

Jill has also received healing within this community of Christians. "For me the *process* of healing has been long, sometimes painful, challenging and strenuous." She realizes how deeply she needs the commitment and accountability of others, how much she needs them to shed light on areas of darkness in her heart and mind. "It was the community that encouraged me to face my pain, forgive myself and be real."

Jill tells about a church retreat that helped her healing process: "As I walked, I had a clear picture in my mind of my heart as a tiny little piece of charcoal. Jesus came to me with a beautiful clear glass box and in that box was a satin pillow with a solid gold heart. He stood there and handed it to me. He didn't say anything, but I knew he was calling me to let go of the pain, to give him my old black heart and to take the brand new heart."

Later that day, she asked some members of her church to pray with her. She wept for the mistakes she had made in her adultery and divorce. One of them said to her, "I see your life as a jigsaw puzzle. You have been trying so hard to put it together yourself and the pieces just aren't fitting quite right. I see Christ taking those pieces and lovingly placing them in the frame of your life so they fit. It may not be the picture you imagined, but Jesus is here to put the pieces in right."

With the help of the community of faith and the healing work of Jesus, Jill is building a rich, full and whole life. We can, too! We can build our lives day by day. Our ongoing struggle with the temptations we face can facilitate a growth process that moves us through forgiveness toward freedom and holiness.

Appendix: Prayers of Confession

Book of Common Prayer[1]

1. Holy God, heavenly Father, you formed me from the dust in your image and likeness, and redeemed me from sin and death by the cross of your Son Jesus Christ. Through the water of baptism you clothed me with the shining garment of his righteousness, and established me among your children in your kingdom. But I have squandered the inheritance of your saints, and have wandered far in a land that is waste.

Especially, I confess to you and to the Church . . .

Here the penitent confesses particular sins.

Therefore, O Lord, from these and all other sins I cannot now remember, I turn to you in sorrow and repentance. Receive me again into the arms of your mercy, and restore me to the blessed company of your faithful people; through him in whom you have redeemed the world, your Son our Savior Jesus Christ. *Amen.*

* * *

2. Most merciful Father, we humbly confess that we have sinned against you in thought, word and deed, by what we have done and by what we have left undone. We have not loved you with our whole heart. We have not loved our neighbors as ourselves. We are truly sorry, and we humbly repent. For the sake of your Son Jesus Christ, have mercy on us and forgive us that we may delight in your will and walk in your ways to the glory of your name. *Amen.*

* * *

3. Almighty God, give us grace to cast away the works of darkness, and put on the armor of light, now in the time of this mortal life in which your Son Jesus Christ came to visit us in great humility; that in the last day, when he shall come again in his glorious majesty to judge both the living and the dead, we may rise to the life immortal; through him who lives and reigns with you and the Holy Spirit, one God, now and for ever. *Amen.*

* * *

4. Purify our conscience, Almighty God, by your daily visitation, that your Son Jesus Christ, at his coming, may find in us a mansion prepared for himself; who lives and reigns with you, in the unity of the Holy Spirit, one God, now and for ever. *Amen.*

* * *

5. Almighty God, whose blessed Son was led by the Spirit to be tempted by Satan: Come quickly to help us who are assaulted by many temptations; and, as you know the weaknesses of each of us, let each one find you mighty to save; through Jesus Christ your Son our Lord, who lives and reigns with you and the Holy Spirit, one God, now and for ever. *Amen.*

* * *

6. O God, whose glory it is always to have mercy: Be gracious to all who have gone astray from your ways, and bring them again with penitent hearts and steadfast faith to embrace and hold fast the unchangeable truth of your Word, Jesus Christ your Son; who with you and the Holy Spirit lives and reigns, one God, for ever and ever. *Amen.*

* * *

7. Almighty God, you know that we have no power in ourselves to help ourselves: Keep us both outwardly in our bodies and inwardly in our

souls, that we may be defended from all adversities which may happen
to the body, and from all evil thoughts which may assault and hurt
the soul; through Jesus Christ our Lord, who lives and reigns with you
and the Holy Spirit, one God, for ever and ever. *Amen.*

* * *

8. Almighty God, you alone can bring into order the unruly wills and
affections of sinners: Grant your people grace to love what you command and desire what you promise; that, among the swift and varied
changes of the world, our hearts may surely there be fixed where true
joys are to be found; through Jesus Christ our Lord, who lives and
reigns with you and the Holy Spirit, one God, now and for ever. *Amen.*

Contemporary Prayer For Public Worship[2]

1. *"Here are words you may trust,*
words that merit full acceptance:
'Christ Jesus came into the world to save sinners.' "

To all who confess their sins
and resolve to lead a new life
he says:
 "Your sins are forgiven,"

and he also says:
 "Follow me."

"Now to the King of all worlds,
immortal, invisible, the only wise God,
be honour and glory for ever and ever. Amen."

* * *

2. *Listen—*
here is good news:
"Christ Jesus came into the world to save sinners"
—to forgive you in your failure

—to accept you as you are
—to set you free from evil's power
and make you what you were meant to be.

Listen to him,
for through him his Father says
to all who come to him, as you have come to him:
    "You are accepted.
    You are forgiven.
    I will set you free."

"O depth of wealth, wisdom, and knowledge in God!
How unsearchable his judgments, how untraceable his ways! . . .
Source, Guide, and Goal of all that is—
to him be glory for ever!
Amen."

Oxford Book of Prayer[3]

1. God in Heaven, you have helped my life to grow like a tree. Now something has happened. Satan, like a bird, has carried in one twig of his own choosing after another. Before I knew it he had built a dwelling place and was living in it. Tonight, my Father, I am throwing out both the bird and the nest. *(Prayer of a Nigerian Christian)*

* * *

2. O thou great Chief, light a candle in my heart, that I may see what is therein, and sweep the rubbish from thy dwelling place. *(An African schoolgirl's prayer)*

* * *

3. Our Father in heaven, I thank thee that thou hast led me into the light. I thank thee for sending the Saviour to call me from death to life. I confess that I was dead in sin before I heard his call, but when I heard him, like Lazarus, I arose. But, O my Father, the grave clothes bind me still. Old habits that I cannot throw off, old customs that are so much a part of my life that I am helpless to live the new life that Christ calls me to live. Give me strength, O Father, to break the bonds; give me courage to live a new life in thee; give me faith, to believe that with thy help I cannot fail. And this I ask in the Saviour's name who has taught me to come to thee. *(Prayer from Taiwan)*

* * *

4. From the cowardice that dare not face new truth
From the laziness that is contented with half truth
From the arrogance that thinks it knows all truth,
Good Lord, deliver me. (Prayer from Kenya)

* * *

5. Look upon us and hear us, O Lord our God; and assist those endeavours to please thee which thou thyself hast granted to us; as thou hast given the first act of will, so give the completion of the work; grant that we may be able to finish what thou hast granted us to wish to begin; through Jesus Christ our Lord. *(Mozarabic)*

* * *

6. May the love of the Lord Jesus
   draw us to himself;
May the power of the Lord Jesus
   strengthen us in his service;
May the joy of the Lord Jesus
   fill our souls.
May the blessing of God almighty,
   the Father, the Son, and the Holy Ghost,
   be amongst you
   and remain with you
      always.
(William Temple, 1881-1944)

Book of Common Prayer

1. Grant us, Lord, not to be anxious about earthly things, but to love things heavenly; and even now, while we are placed among things

that are passing away, to hold fast to those that shall endure; through Jesus Christ our Lord, who lives and reigns with you and the Holy Spirit, one God, for ever and ever. *Amen.*

* * *

2. Almighty and everlasting God, you are always more ready to hear than we to pray, and to give more than we either desire or deserve: Pour upon us the abundance of your mercy, forgiving us those things of which our conscience is afraid, and giving us those good things for which we are not worthy to ask, except through the merits and mediation of Jesus Christ our Savior; who lives and reigns with you and the Holy Spirit, one God, for ever and ever. *Amen.*

Notes

Chapter 1

[1]Epiphanus, quoted in Janice Nunnally-Cox, *Foremothers: Women of the Bible* (New York: Seabury, 1981), p. 152.

[2]Carol Gilligan, *In a Different Voice: Psychological Theory and Women's Development* (Cambridge, Mass.: Harvard University Press, 1982), p. 18.

[3]Nancy Chodorow, *The Reproduction of Mothering: Psychoanalysis and the Sociology of Gender* (Berkeley: University of California Press, 1978).

[4]Gilbert Bilezikian, *Beyond Sex Roles: What the Bible Says about Woman's Place in Church and Family* (Grand Rapids: Baker, 1989), p. 3.

[5]Mary Stewart Van Leeuwen, "The Christian Mind and the Challenge of Gender Relations," *The Reformed Journal,* Sept. 1987.

[6]Nunnally-Cox, *Foremothers,* p. 152.

[7]Letty Cottin Pogrebin, *Growing Up Free: Raising Your Child in the 80's* (New York: McGraw, 1980), p. 398.

[8]Mary Field Belenky, Blythe McVicker Clinchy, Nancy Rule Goldberger, and Jill Mattuck Tarule, *Women's Ways of Knowing: The Development of Self, Voice, and Mind* (New York: Basic Books, 1986).

[9]Nunnally-Cox, *Foremothers,* p. 153.

[10]Ibid., p. 152.

[11]Larry Christenson, *The Christian Family* (Minneapolis: Bethany, 1970), pp. 35-37.

[12]Bilezikian, *Beyond Sex Roles,* p. 81.

[13]Mary Evans, *Woman in the Bible* (Downers Grove, Ill.: InterVarsity Press, 1984), p. 44.

Chapter 2

[1]*Time,* March 5, 1990, p. 59; and October 22, 1990, p. 59.

[2]Judith Plaskow, *Sex, Sin, and Grace: Women's Experience and the Theologies of Reinhold Niebuhr and Paul Tillich* (Washington: University Press of America, 1980), p. 77.

[3]Carolyn Heilbrun, *Writing a Woman's Life* (New York: Norton, 1988), pp. 22-23.

[4]Jürgen Moltmann, *Theology of Hope* (New York: Harper & Row, 1975), p. 22.

[5]Gilligan, *In a Different Voice,* p. 120.

[6]Linda T. Sanford and Mary Ellen Donovan, *Women and Self-Esteem* (New York: Penguin, 1985), p. 6.

[7]Belenky et al., *Women's Ways of Knowing,* p. 6.

[8]Sanford and Donovan, *Women and Self-Esteem,* p. 6.

[9]Irene H. Frieze, *Women and Sex Roles: A Social Psychological Perspective* (New York: Norton, 1978), p. 245.

[10]Collette Dowling, *Perfect Women* (New York: Summit, 1988), p. 72.

Chapter 3

[1]Gerard Hughes, *God of Surprises* (Mahway, N. J., Paulist Press, 1986), p. 56.

[2]Harriet Goldhor Lerner, *The Dance of Intimacy: A Woman's Guide to Courageous Acts of Change in Key Relationships* (New York: Harper & Row, 1989), pp. 186-87.

[3]Henri Nouwen, *Lifesigns: Intimacy, Fecundity, and Ecstasy in Christian Perspective* (New York: Doubleday, 1986), pp. 57-74.

Chapter 4

[1]Jacques Ellul, *Money and Power* (Downers Grove, Ill.: InterVarsity Press, 1984), pp. 82-84.

[2]Laura Ingalls Wilder, *Little House in the Big Woods* (New York: Harper & Row, 1971), p. 170.

[3]Wiley, Kim Wright, "The Mystique of Money," *Savvy,* April 1987, p. 34.

[4]Ibid.

[5]Dowling, *Perfect Women,* p. 49.

[6]Richard Foster, *Freedom of Simplicity* (San Francisco: Harper & Row, 1981), p. 118.

Chapter 5

[1]Dowling, *Perfect Women,* p. 53.

[2]Sanford and Donovan, *Women and Self-Esteem,* p. 370.

[3]Dowling, *Perfect Women,* pp. 14, 28.

[4]Carol Christ, *Diving Deep and Surfacing* (Boston: Beacon, 1980), p. 16.

[5]Kim Chernin, *The Obsession: Reflections on the Tyranny of Slenderness* (New York: Harper & Row, 1981), p. 155.

[6]Julie Johnson, "Bringing Sanity to the Diet Craze," *Time,* 21 May 1990, p. 74.

[7]Willard Harley, *His Needs, Her Needs: Building an Affair-Proof Marriage* (Old Tappan, N. J.: Revell, 1986), pp. 101-2.

[8]Dorothy L. Sayers, *Are Women Human?* (Grand Rapids: Eerdmans, 1971), p. 22.

[9]C. S. Lewis, *The Screwtape Letters* (New York: Macmillan, 1982), p. 57.

Chapter 6

[1]P. T. Forsyth, quoted in Charles E. Hummel, *The Tyranny of the Urgent* (Downers Grove, Ill., InterVarsity Press, 1967).

[2]Roberta Hestenes, "Scripture and the Ministry of Women within the Church Community," in *Women and the Ministries of Christ,* ed. Roberta Hestenes and Lois Curley (Pasadena: Fuller Theological Seminary, 1979), p. 64.

[3]Roberta Hestenes, personal interview, April 1989.

[4]Nouwen, *Lifesigns,* p. 49.

[5]Joyce Huggett, *The Joy of Listening to God* (Downers Grove, Ill.: InterVarsity Press, 1986).

Chapter 7

[1]Louise Eichenbaum and Susie Orbach, *Between Women* (New York: Viking, 1988), p. 135.

[2]Harriet Goldhor Lerner, *The Dance of Anger* (New York: Harper & Row, 1985). pp. 1-2, 9.

[3]Irina Ratushinskaya, *Grey Is the Color of Hope* (New York: Vintage International, 1989), pp. 260-61.

Chapter 8

[1]Dorothy Sayers, "The Other Six Deadly Sins," *The Whimsical Christian* (New York: Collier/Macmillan, 1987), p. 157.

[2]Ruth Sidel, *On Her Own: Growing Up in the Shadow of the American Dream* (New York: Viking, 1990).

[3]Evelyn Eaton Weatherhead and James D. Weatherhead, *A Sense of Sexuality: Christian Love and Intimacy* (New York: Doubleday, 1989), p. 195.

[4]M. Scott Peck, *The Road Less Traveled: A New Psychology of Love, Traditional Values, and Spiritual Growth* (New York: Simon and Schuster, 1978), pp. 84-93.

[5]Weatherhead and Weatherhead, *A Sense of Sexuality,* p. 197.

[6]Kevin Diaz, "No Love Lost in the Dating Business," *Minneapolis Star Tribune,* July 5, 1990, pp. 1E-9E.

[7]Jennifer Logan, *Not Just Any Man: A Guide to Finding Mr. Right* (Waco, Tex.: Word, 1989), p. 96.

[8]Ibid., p. 85.

[9]Ibid., p. 131.

[10]Ibid., p. 162.

[11]Ibid., p. 171.

[12]Ibid.

[13]Weatherhead and Weatherhead, *A Sense of Sexuality,* p. 217.

[14]Ibid., p. 218.

[15]Elaine Storkey, *What's Right with Feminism* (Grand Rapids: Eerdmans, 1985), p. 175.

[16]Letha Scanzoni and Nancy Hardesty, *All We're Meant to Be: A Biblical Approach to Women's Liberation* (Waco, Tex.: Word, 1974) p. 148.

[17]Evelyn Bence, "The Desires of Thine Heart," Priscilla Papers, 4 (Spring 1990), pp. 8-10.

Chapter 9

[1]Weatherhead and Weatherhead, *A Sense of Sexuality,* p. 26.

[2]Ibid.

[3]Lewis Smedes, *Sex for Christians* (Grand Rapids: Eerdmans, 1976), p. 47.

[4]Augustine, *City of God,* quoted in Richard Foster, *Money, Sex, and Power: The Challenge of the Disciplined Life* (San Francisco: Harper & Row, 1985), p. 100.

[5]Weatherhead and Weatherhead, *A Sense of Sexuality,* pp. 97-98.

[6]Dale Spender, *Man-Made Language* (London: Rutledge and Kegan Paul, 1985), p. 178.

[7]Paul D. Meier, Frank B. Minirth, and Frank B. Wichern, *Introduction to Psychology and Counseling: Christian Perspectives and Applications* (Grand Rapids: Baker, 1982), p. 372.

[8]Ibid., p. 373.

[9]Harley, *His Needs, Her Needs,* p. 41.

[10]Foster, *Money, Sex, and Power,* p. 140.

[11]Weatherhead and Weatherhead, *A Sense of Sexuality,* p. 33.

Chapter 10

[1]Betsy Cohen, *The Snow White Syndrome: All About Envy* (New York: Macmillan, 1986), p. 21.

²Ibid., pp. 17-19.
³Eichenbaum and Orbach, *Between Women*, p. 108.

Chapter 11
¹Harry Blamires, *Recovering the Christian Mind: The Challenge of Secularism* (Downers Grove, Ill.: InterVarsity Press, 1988), p. 134.
²Hughes, *God of Surprises*, p. 34.
³Nouwen, *Lifesigns*, p. 21.
⁴Ross Campbell, *How to Really Love Your Child* (Wheaton, Ill.: Victor Books, 1979).

Chapter 12
¹Nouwen, *Lifesigns*, p. 92.
²Erwin Ramsdell Goodenough, *The Psychology of Religious Experience* (New York: Basic Books, 1965), pp. 102-3.

Chapter 13
¹Nouwen, *Lifesigns*, p. 67.
²John White, *The Fight* (Downers Grove, Ill.: InterVarsity Press, 1976), pp. 85-86.

Chapter 14
¹Lerner, *The Dance of Intimacy*, p. 35.
²Robert Bellah et al., *Habits of the Heart: Individualism and Commitment in American Life* (Berkeley: University of California Press, 1985), pp. 226, 228.
³Eichenbaum and Orbach, *Between Women*, pp. 53-54.
⁴Ibid., p. 63.
⁵Ibid., p. 62.
⁶Nouwen, *Lifesigns*, p. 36.

Appendix
¹*The Book of Common Prayer of the Episcopal Church* (New York: Church Hymnal Corporation, 1977).
²Caryl Michlen, ed., *Contemporary Prayer for Public Worship* (London: SCM, 1967).
³George Appleton, ed., *The Oxford Book of Prayer* (Oxford: Oxford University Press, 1985).